Sunset

Herbs
AN ILLUSTRATED GUIDE

By the Editors of Sunset Books and Sunset Magazine

*Billowy softness of lavender cotton, an herb-garden favorite since
Elizabethan times, belies its rugged constitution.*

Sunset Publishing Corporation
Menlo Park, California

Foxglove

Research & Text
Philip Edinger

Coordinating Editor
Suzanne Normand Eyre

Design
Sandra Popovich

Illustrations
Lois Lovejoy

A CONTEMPORY HERBAL

It's no wonder that herbs have never lost their popularity. For thousands of years, their beauty, fragrance, and flavor have given humankind much pleasure. Moreover, herbs were our first medicines, used to treat problems ranging from sore throats and hypertension to heart disease and battle wounds.

Today, we season our foods with culinary herbs, prepare scents from the aromatic kinds, and, of course, cultivate them for the color and texture they bring to the garden. Even herbal medicine is experiencing a renaissance as scientific research confirms in the laboratory what our ancestors knew from experience.

On the following pages you'll encounter herbs from an historical perspective and learn how to grow them. Illustrated profiles of the most common types explain each herb's cultivation requirements and uses, and a final chapter describes products you can make from the herbs you grow.

We extend our thanks to Karyn Lipman for her assistance with the recipes and to Fran Feldman for her meticulous copyediting.

Photographers

Scott Atkinson: 30, 31, 110 left; **Liz Ball, Photo/Nats:** 67, 88, 90; **Cathy Wilkinson Barash, Photo/Nats:** 86; **Glenn Christiansen:** 16; **Rosalind Creasy:** 43, 68, 89, 100, 106, 110 right; **Derek Fell:** 10 left, 15 right, 36, 39, 46, 47, 51, 53, 54, 69, 70, 94; **Betsy Fuchs, Photo/Nats:** 76; **Harry Haralambou:** 14 right, 28, 34, 50, 102; **Saxon Holt:** 3, 10 right, 15 left, 56, 57, 61, 65, 77, 92, 98; **Horticultural Photography:** 48, 73, 97; **Jerry Pavia:** 6, 14 left, 17, 32, 35, 41, 58, 59, 83; **Joanne Pavia:** 4, 52, 93, 95; **Ann Reilly, Photo/Nats:** 1, 44, 62, 66, 91; **Michael S. Thompson:** 24, 37, 38, 60, 63, 71, 74, 75, 79, 81, 84, 87, 96, 107; **Virginia Twinam-Smith, Photo/Nats:** 55, 78; **Darrow M. Watt:** 103, 105, 108; **Cynthia Woodyard:** 11, 12, 40, 42, 45, 49, 80, 82, 85, 99; **Barbara Worl:** 9; **Tom Wyatt:** 104; **Josephine Zeitlin:** 7, 8.

Editor, Sunset Books: Elizabeth L. Hogan

Second printing March 1994

Cover: *Mixed planting showcases three favorite herbs: French lavender, chives, and spearmint. Cover design by Susan Bryant. Photography by Cynthia Woodyard.*

CONTENTS

Both foliage and flowers offer colorful accents in this chartreuse-leafed variant of feverfew.

THE LORE & LURE OF HERBS

Humankind has relied on herbs since before the time of recorded history. The earliest records of useful herbs testify to practices that already were traditional. In day-to-day living, herbs served as medicine, first-aid relief, food and seasoning, cosmetics, and dyes. In religious practices, they provided talismans, mind-altering substances for priestly divinations, ceremonial offerings, and materials for embalming. Even toxic herbs had a place — in warfare, where they poisoned the enemy, and for protection from marauding animals that threatened safety or food supplies.

Today, herbs are used in many of the same ways, though we may not always recognize their presence. Consider this as you drink your morning cup of tea or rub on your favorite lotion. . . .

For thousands of years, herbs have been the basis for medicine, magic, and menu planning. Here, a traditional setting displays a variety of herbs within a framework of boxwood.

WHAT IS AN HERB?

Trying to define the word "herb" can provoke lively discussion. In truth, no one definition will let you easily establish categories of herbs and non-herbs. Three separate definitions illustrate the problem — and give an indication of the diversity of plants covered by the word.

In dictionaries, you'll find "herb" defined first as an annual, biennial, or perennial seed-producing plant that dies down at the end of each growing season, as opposed to a tree or shrub that has woody stems and lives for more than a year. This definition embraces many of the familiar culinary herbs but fails to include such favorite seasoning plants as shrubby rosemary and treelike bay. But more important, it includes all plants botanically termed "herbaceous": all annuals, the majority of bulbous plants (tulips as herbs?), and many favorite perennials grown solely for their beauty.

A second definition generally narrows the field to a plant (or plant parts) that is used for seasoning, scent, or medicine. But this explanation, though closer to what we might expect, still excludes plants used for cosmetics or dyes, or for ritual purposes.

The American Herb Society resolves the question by avoiding specifics, officially declaring that an herb is "any plant that can be used for pleasure, fragrance, or physic." You still can't size up an unfamiliar plant and say, "Aha, that's an herb." But neither can you say, without a bit of research, that it isn't. The very fuzziness of this definition lets us include all plants that have historic or current use in any of the ways mentioned on the previous page.

Two questions remain. What, if anything, distinguishes spices from herbs? Specifically, a spice is generally defined as an aromatic plant that can be used to add flavor to foods and beverages. Defining "spice" in this manner throws together what may appear to be some rather odd companions: such grow-at-home seasonings as basil, oregano, and thyme and such exotic imports as cinnamon, cloves, and nutmeg. But under the American Herb Society definition, all of the above technically qualify as herbs precisely because they're used for pleasure (taste) and fragrance. "Spice," then, is a word that covers culinary herbs in the broadest sense.

The final question is the matter of pronunciation. Is it "herb" or "erb"? The answer is that it's both. In the British Isles (and in some former British colonies), you sound the "h"; in the United States, the "h" remains silent.

An herb sampler shows the diversity among familiar plants: perennial sage, fennel, green lavender cotton, and woody rosemary. Unclipped boxwood forms the backdrop.

HERBS:
THEIR EARLY HISTORY

The world's most ancient civilizations gathered, grew, and used herbs. Earliest records of civilizations from the Tigris/Euphrates region to China refer to herbs used for their taste, fragrance, or medicinal qualities.

The oldest existing, authentic mention of herbs may be an Egyptian document, written on a papyrus scroll, dating from about 1550 B.C. The text was medical and among the useful plants recorded were many of our most familiar herbs, such as anise, caraway, fennel, and garlic.

Two Chinese medical texts that also mentioned herbs were thought to be about a thousand years older than the Egyptian papyrus document, though current scholarship suggests a later date instead. Regardless of which culture can claim first publication status, the important point is that the Chinese tradition of herbal medicine obviously dates to before the time of written records. Remarkably, that medical tradition continues to this very day.

The earliest accounts discussing herbs in any abundance stem from the cultures of ancient Greece and, later, Rome. Myths surrounding gods and goddesses abound with references to herbs that were sacred to, or favorites of, a particular deity; the origin of one herb, mint, was even attributed to divine intervention.

Four surviving scholarly texts, three Greek and one Roman, provide us with the best historical evidence today of herb growing and use in ancient times. One author was Theophrastus, of Eresus on the Greek island Lesbos, who studied with both Plato and Aristotle during the third century B.C., thus benefiting from the best education available at the time. He put this fine background to work in producing what can be considered the first botany book, *Historia Plantarum*, the greatest influence in Western plant study for more than a thousand years. For the many plants he included, he furnished information on what each looked like,

According to ancient Greek legend, mullein was an antidote to certain evil spirits. During the Middle Ages, its stalks were used as torches.

where it was found, and what its uses were. By classifying plants into four groups — trees, shrubs, half-shrubs, and herbs (growth dying to the ground each year) — he established distinctions that we still rely on today.

Another surviving work, that of the Roman historian Gaius Plinius Secundus, usually known as Pliny the Elder, comes several hundred years later. Born in 23 A.D., Pliny the Elder met a dramatic end in the 79 A.D. eruption of Vesuvius, which destroyed Pompeii and Herculaneum. But before that fateful event, he studied the natural world in its broadest sense — astronomy, meteorology, geography, as well as flora and fauna — and condensed this knowledge into a book called *Natural History*. In this work, Pliny described individual plants, their most pertinent distinctions and uses, and their growth and habits.

At about the same time, two Greek physicians were also advancing the knowledge of herbs. Dioscorides, who lived in the first century A.D., was a physician with the Roman armies and traveled widely in their campaigns. His five-volume work on *materia medica* described countless medications derived from local plants.

Galen (Claudius Galenus, 131 to 201 A.D.) was a high-ranking physician in imperial Rome who wrote voluminously on a wide range of subjects. Quite naturally, medicine was among them and the medications he cited were, in large part, derived from plants.

One other fertile source of information on herbs in ancient times is, of course, the Bible, particularly the Old Testament. Even though some of the plant names mentioned don't correspond with plants of those names today, abundant references attest to the importance of herbs in religious practices and everyday life.

HERBS IN THE DARK AGES

During the centuries — often referred to as the Dark Ages — that intervened between the fall of the Roman Empire and the stirrings of the Renaissance, knowledge in the Western world was preserved and passed along chiefly in European monasteries. Records and plans from those religious enclaves clearly show "physic gardens" in which were grown the various herbs used in treating wounds and ailments.

At the same time that agents of the Church kept the flame of knowledge burning, another body of herbal lore was perpetuated by the common people. Transmitted orally from generation to generation, this body of information dealt with herbs used not only for health purposes but also for witchcraft, spells, and talismans.

Two notable forces advanced the knowledge of herbs outside the religious cloisters during this period. Under the direction of Charlemagne (742–814), the Holy Roman Emperor, gardens were established throughout his domain according to quite specific instructions about choice of plants to be cultivated: usefulness for food, medicine, or household function was the sole criterion.

At about the same time, the rise of Islam in Arabia and its subsequent spread throughout the Middle East, North Africa, and Spain brought highly developed Arabic medical practices, derived from the Greco-Roman tradition, to regions where the ancient herbal knowledge would later enter the European mainstream.

Contemporary garden (at The Cloisters in New York City) provides a medieval setting for a period herb garden featuring lovage, tansy, and horseradish.

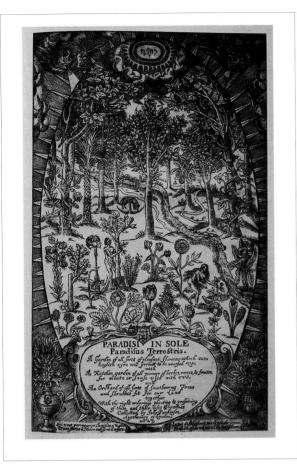

The herbals presented botany, natural history, gardening, medicine, cooking, and more. Shown is the title page from John Parkinson's Paridisi in Sole Paradisus Terrestris *(1629).*

THE FLOWERING OF THE HERBALS

As Western Europe progressed from tribal culture to powerful city-states, commerce accelerated. The Renaissance began. And early in the Renaissance, two events furthered the knowledge and use of herbs. The first was the 13th-century journey of the Polo brothers and young Marco from Venice to China and back. They returned with herbs and spices that whetted European appetites for more. Thus began an active spice trade that enlarged and enriched the European store of herbs.

The second, and more important, development was the invention of the printing press.

What formerly had to be copied by hand — generally in the monasteries — could now be produced in quantity. This resulted in the proliferation and spread of books containing botanical information, medical remedies, recipes, and household tips. Those books, called "herbals," typically contained descriptions of all useful plants known to the writer, information on where to grow them, their supposed compatibility with one another, and any peculiarities of harvesting, use, and propagation. Included in the author's personal observations were lore from ancient writers or other herbalists, hearsay, and superstition.

We now know that gems of truth are embedded in the herbal texts. But the content of hearsay and superstition made for some pretty fantastic claims, at least by today's standards. The most unusual assertions concerned herbs' medical and spiritual uses. One approach to medicine promoted the Doctrine of Signatures, which held that if any part of a plant resembled a body part or organ, it was effective in treating that part. Plants were then named accordingly. Thus, lungwort (*Pulmonaria*), whose spotted leaves supposedly resembled diseased lungs, was thought to cure chest ailments. Eyebright (*Euphrasia officinalis*), with its flowers that looked like bloodshot eyes, was called on to treat cataracts and blindness. The herbs selfheal and heal-all were the first of their genre, the snake-oil remedies.

Diagnosis and cure by astrology was another approach to medicine. Each herb was associated with one of the seven planets known at the time and also with one of the signs of the zodiac. In addition, parts of the body were assigned to planetary and zodiacal dominion. Remedies were a matter of using the herb whose planet and sign were sympathetic or strengthening to the affected body part.

The strongly held religious faith of the time gave rise to herbs that would repel evil spirits, the evil eye, and other malevolent forces. Interestingly, herbal love potions flourished in the same atmosphere.

Several of the European herbals were notable for their quality of information, fidelity of botanical illustration, or both. Those of Otto Brunfels and Leonhard Fuchs (both German) and Rembert Dodoens (Dutch) are preeminent. But mention of the word "herbal" usually brings to mind three Englishmen who produced enormously popular (if not always enormously factual) herbals in the period from 1597 to 1650.

The earliest of these was John Gerard's *Herball or Generall Historie of Plantes*, published in 1597 and revised in 1633 after the author's death. It combines good botanical observation with medical advice and a comparative minimum of fanciful material. In 1640, John Parkinson produced *Theatrum Botanicum*, an ambitious work that describes nearly 4,000 plants from Europe, Asia, and the New World. The book borrows material from other herbals and illustrations from Gerard.

The most popular herbal, though replete with highly imaginative information, was that of Nicholas Culpepper. His goal in *The English Physician* was to create a family medical text, a guidebook to home diagnosis and cure. But because he was a firm believer in the Doctrine of

Signatures and astrological medicine, Culpepper's herbal is largely of historical rather than scientific interest.

HERBS IN HOUSE & GARDEN

In addition to their importance as medicinal plants during the Middle Ages and the Renaissance, herbs were used for their fragrances, flavors, and decorative value.

In times when bathing and even fresh air were considered unhealthful, pleasant fragrances could mask the aromas of everyday life. Certain herbs were valued for "strewing" — placing on floors where they would be walked upon, thus releasing their fragrances into the air. Nosegays, fragrant herbs wrapped in pieces of cloth, offered portable

Medieval-style herb garden (at left) features geometric beds, paved pathways, and classical statuary. Freeform knot garden (above) relies on lavender, germander, lavender cotton, and boxwood, accented by dwarf red-leaf Japanese barberry.

and instant aromatherapy. Some herbs were thought to have disinfectant power, able even to ward off disease.

And, of course, herbs were used as foods and seasonings, though in different ways from present-day cooking. Old recipes and cookbooks show that foods were more highly seasoned then than now. Because meats especially were often in some state of spoilage, heavy seasoning was needed to disguise or overpower the flavor and scent of decay. Often, an Elizabethan salad would contain more than 30 different kinds of leaves, roots, seeds, and vegetables, collectively referred to as "salet herbs." Many of the plants familiar to us as vegetables were then considered herbs and were eaten for their supposed health-giving qualities.

For the wealthy few, the Renaissance meant greater leisure to indulge in learning and the arts. An outgrowth was the concept of gardens designed purely for pleasure. No longer were herbs cultivated just by monks, apothecaries, and cooks. Instead, those familiar plants, along with others, took their place in decorative situations. Walled gardens with geometric beds were a natural start, considering the need for security. But soon, more romantic and fanciful designs evolved, spawning elaborate knot gardens (see page 19), sundial gardens (in which plants that opened and closed at different times of day were grown in a circular bed), thyme- and chamomile-planted walks and earthen seats, checkerboard plantings of low herbs in contrasting colors, and the like.

In the style of an English country garden, this home landscape features diverse herbs, including foxglove, lavenders, mullein, pinks (not yet in flower), and wormwood.

THE ROLE OF HERBS TODAY

With modern scientific analysis, it's now possible to isolate and identify the "active ingredients" of herbs; in the process, people are learning that much ancient wisdom and many folk remedies do, indeed, have a firm basis for effectiveness. Foxglove, from which an important heart medicine is derived, is a sterling example. But today, most gardeners grow herbs for their culinary uses, their colorful histories, and their beauty (for some modern-day uses of herbs, see the chapter beginning on page 101).

Growing herbs, then, is almost purely a matter of pleasure, with no practical constraints imposed on design. Gardeners are free to borrow from any tradition, including knot garden, medieval cloister garden, Colonial kitchen garden, English country garden, and Southwestern xeriscape planting. And, of course, many have discovered the beauty of herbs when interspersed among purely ornamental plants.

INTRODUCING HERBS TO THE GARDEN

Whether you intend to use your herbs or you simply want them for their historical, visual, and olfactory appeal, you'll find countless ways to display them attractively in the garden. Foliage ranges from the filigree of fennel to the tiny leaves of Corsican mint to the butter paddles of comfrey; colors may be silvery gray, chartreuse, bronze, or variegated, as well as all shades of green. Some herbs even produce showy blossoms. Growth habits run the gamut from ground-hugging mats to upright spires.

Clearly, herbs offer garden possibilities limited only by imagination. And that's a beauty of herbs: there are no set rules for planting design and combinations. Let the following pages inspire you as you plant your own unique herb garden.

Herbs become prominent features in an otherwise traditional landscape. Bronze fennel clumps provide upright, feathery accent points; lavender cotton spreads its billowy gray foliage in the foreground.

PLANNING
AN HERB GARDEN

Like any other project you undertake, your garden is likely to give greater satisfaction if you invest a bit of time in planning before you start digging.

PURPOSE. Think first of all about what kind of herb planting you want. Many new herb growers, aiming for a planting that will be useful as well as interesting, gravitate toward the culinary herbs. But you might just as easily decide to collect an assortment of medicinal herbs or concentrate on plants common in medieval apothecary gardens. An even narrower focus would concentrate just on, say, the many mints or oreganos.

Deciding on your purpose lets you focus on a group of plants, gets you acquainted with the variables in their growths and appearances, gives you a slant on their garden needs, and allows you to start listing the ones you want.

CULTURAL NEEDS. While many herbs may be content with average soil and moderate water, their individual needs are diverse enough to frustrate generalization. As you decide what herbs you want to grow, check the cultural information for each plant (see the section beginning on page 33) to be sure you're planning a compatible assortment. Keep the "sunshine set" separate from the shade-and-moisture lovers.

SOIL. If you're used to catering to the needs of roses or preparing the annual vegetable plot, you'll put the majority of herbs in the unfussy, easy-care category. Nevertheless, if you plan to grow herbs where nothing has been planted before, do a bit of soil preparation first (for help, see page 26). Even the most carefree plants will perform better if the soil is made hospitable to root growth.

TYPES OF
PLANTINGS

Mention of the phrase "herb garden" may evoke an image of carefully laid-out beds with plants growing neatly in their assigned positions. But, in truth, herbs can be incorporated into a garden in any number of ways, from exclusive to occasional and from simple to elaborate.

Plantings may focus on visual interest, as in the lavender-rue-wormwood combination at left, or emphasize culinary utility, as shown above in a garden of thymes, sage, and chives.

A traditional garden framework (at left) mixes herbs with ornamentals and potted lemons in an outdoor-living area. Thyme-nestled paving stones (below) meander through a planting of woolly betony (lamb's ears), nasturtiums, yarrow, and wormwood.

HERBS EXCLUSIVELY. In this traditional herb-garden approach, you may consign the entire garden space to herbs of one sort or another, or you can create a garden within a garden — an herb knot garden, for example, used as an accent in a nonherb landscape.

HERBS AMONG OTHER PLANTS. Think of this type of planting as the cottage-garden concept, in which plants are combined according to pleasing appearance rather than segregated into separate groups according to their functions. Contemporary edible gardens that combine vegetables in plantings of purely ornamental plants often incorporate culinary herbs. In the same spirit, many attractive but nonedible herbs can find their way into mixed plantings of annuals, perennials, and flowering shrubs.

HERBS UNDERFOOT. Several low and spreading herbs are resilient enough to withstand light foot traffic. Chamomile "lawns" have a history that extends back at least to Elizabethan times, their worthiness noted by Shakespeare's Falstaff. And chamomile plants (*Chamaemelum nobile* and its named selections), as well as flat-to-the-ground mints (*Mentha pulegium*, *M. requienii*) and woolly thyme, will grow well between loosely laid paving stones, softening the hard edges and releasing pleasant scents with each footfall.

HERB GROUND COVERS. One step above the lawn and crevice herbs are a number of low-growing plants that you can mass for small-scale ground cover or even plant among thick paving stones for a fairly frowzy path. Various thymes and oreganos are first-rate, attractive subjects for mass planting, as is germander.

Prostrate rosemary (*Rosmarinus officinalis* 'Prostratus'), though it eventually builds to about 2 feet high without restraint, can be kept low with periodic trimming. A regular going-over with hedge shears will keep its surface nearly as flat as a tabletop.

HERB HEDGES. The tightly clipped herb ribbons that delineate knot gardens are really miniature hedges. Lavender cotton and germander are favorite plants for this rigid control; they're just as effective used as low border hedges in less-intricate contexts. The low-growing lavenders also make effective edging plants; give them just one annual shearing in early spring and let them develop naturally for the rest of the year.

If you need taller plants for the backdrop of your planting, choose an upright rosemary, such as *Rosmarinus officinalis* 'Tuscan Blue', or bush germander; these can be sheared often enough to keep the effect formal. For a more informal appearance, turn to English lavender and its hybrids.

HERB BENCHES. An Elizabethan fancy, the herb bench is a garden seat planted with prostrate herbs that, when sat upon, release their fragrances. In essence, such benches are planters built to bench height and containing just enough soil depth to satisfy the roots of the herbs.

Stone, brick, concrete block, and wood are all appropriate materials for such a structure. The best herbs for bench planting are those listed for herb lawns (see "Herbs Underfoot" on page 15).

HERB DRY WALLS. Mortarless stone walls, where soil pockets exist between stones, make good-looking showplaces for a variety of the low-growing herbs that prefer warmth, good drainage, and moderate water.

Look for good wall plants among the various thymes, catmints, oreganos, and wormwoods. Given a bit of shade (and more moisture), violets will grow easily between stones.

HERBS IN CONTAINERS. Many of the most popular herbs adapt easily to life in containers. For the grower with limited garden space — and for anyone who wants to grow just a few herbs — containers offer a simple solution.

In cold-winter regions, containers provide the only means of maintaining, from one year to the next, a number of somewhat tender, shrubby herbs, such as bay, lemon verbena, rosemary, and scented geraniums. As soon as frosty autumn weather arrives, move these plants indoors or into a greenhouse for the winter.

But containers are more than simple problem-solvers. You can use them as decorative statements, especially when you plant a large container with more than one herb. Large terra-cotta pots (including strawberry jars) will effectively display various herbs for close-up enjoyment on patios and decks; even hanging containers made of clay, wood, or wire can house small herbs. Wooden planters can be constructed to any size you desire; freestanding or as window boxes, they can host small herb collections.

For complete information on growing herbs in containers, turn to pages 28–29.

A simple rustic basket lined with plastic (drainage holes were punched in the bottom) and filled with potting soil makes a bouquetlike herb display.

PLANTING DESIGN

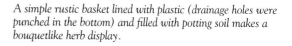

Although there are no hard-and-fast rules regarding design of an herb garden, popular traditions may affect your decisions. And there are some basic guidelines for planting design that should influence your plan. For a look at some typical garden designs that you can re-create in your own style, see pages 18–23.

FORMALITY. Some herb gardens, such as Renaissance knot gardens, are rigidly formal in design. Others, including Colonial-style herb plantings and contemporary "traditional" herb gardens, tend toward a formal design structure even though the plants are not set out in a militarily precise arrangement.

Informal plantings can be equally appealing. The English perennial border — a rectangular bed containing plants carefully arranged so that appearances complement and contrast — serves as a model for an all-herb version that is decidedly informal in effect, though contained within a formal framework. From this approach, it's a short step to the cottage-garden (or its contemporary version, the English country-garden) style, in which an informal arrangement of plants is contained in an irregular or naturalistic planting bed (see page 18).

PLANT RELATIONSHIPS. Unless you plan to grow your herbs in farm-style rows just for harvest, you'll want to consider the overall appearance of the plot or garden you're creating. The old adage that recommends placing tall plants in the back (or in the center, if access is from all sides) is a logical starting point.

But more than simple size needs to be considered. Recognizing the great variations that exist in flowers, leaf colors and textures, and plant sizes and shapes, you can approach your design as a painter might approach a canvas. Employ enough contrast so plants stand out attractively as individuals, but pay attention to complementary relationships that create a pleasing unit rather than a collection of unrelated individuals.

MAINTENANCE. A good design always embraces practical considerations. And for herb plantings, the overriding practical concern is for easy access to the plants.

Whether you set out a naturalistic, easy-care planting or a more labor-intensive knot garden, you'll need to maintain the plants. Trimming and cutting back are common periodic maintenance tasks; setting out new plants — particularly if you're growing annual herbs — is another exercise that may become routine. And with plantings that will yield a crop, you can add harvesting to the list.

Whatever maintenance your herb garden demands, lay out plantings so everything will be within an arm's reach from the area where you'll stand or kneel to do the work. This normally translates to beds no deeper than 3½ feet, if access is just from one side, or to about 7 feet where access is from opposite or all sides. Break up larger plantings with pathways or substantial stepping-stonelike pads.

Combine herbs so their colors and textures complement one another. The garden at left features gray woolly betony (lamb's ears) and violet orris root (Iris pallida). The drought-tolerant planting above shows off mullein with Spanish lavender in the foreground, French lavender behind.

HERB GARDEN PLANS

Although an herb garden can be very compact, as when planted in a strawberry jar, the allure of these varied plants may inspire you to more ambitious ideas that require garden space. The following plans with their variations show you a number of ways, both traditional and contemporary, to incorporate herbs into a garden setting.

INFORMAL GARDEN

1 Rose, Apothecary (*Rosa gallica officinalis*)
2 Lavender, English (*Lavandula angustifolia*)
3 Lavender, dwarf (*Lavandula angustifolia* 'Hidcote')
4 Wormwood (*Artemisia absinthium* 'Lambrook Silver')
5 Rue (*Ruta graveolens*)
6 Sage, purple (*Salvia officinalis* 'Purpurascens')

7 Sage, tricolor (*Salvia officinalis* 'Tricolor')
8 Yarrow, common (*Achillea millefolium*)
9 Fennel, bronze (*Foeniculum vulgare purpureum*)
10 Purple coneflower (*Echinacea purpurea*)
11 Orris root, variegated (*Iris* 'Pallida Variegata')
12 Feverfew, golden (*Chrysanthemum parthenium* 'Aureum')
13 Cottage pink (*Dianthus plumarius*)
14 Catmint (*Nepeta* x *faassenii*)
15 Violet (*Viola odorata*)
16 Self-heal (*Prunella grandiflora*)
17 Burnet (*Poterium sanguisorba*)
18 Betony, woolly (*Stachys byzantina*)
19 Scented geranium, apple- (*Pelargonium odoratissimum*)

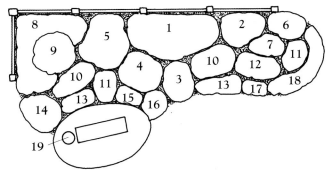

Plan dimensions: 20' x 12'

KNOT GARDEN

Herbs

1 Germander *(Teucrium chamaedrys)*
2 Lavender cotton, green *(Santolina virens)*
3 Lavender cotton *(Santolina chamaecyparissus)*
4 Pot marigold, yellow *(Calendula officinalis)*
5 Pot marigold, cream *(Calendula officinalis)*
6 Sage, variegated *(Salvia officinalis* 'Icterina')

Nonherbs

7 Boxwood, dwarf *(Buxus sempervirens* 'Suffruticosa')
8 Barberry, dwarf red-leaf Japanese *(Berberis thunbergii* 'Crimson Pygmy')

Plan dimensions: 12' x 12'

Alternate patterns

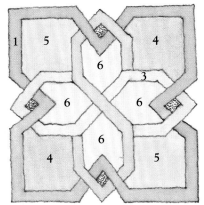

Plan dimensions: 12' x 12'

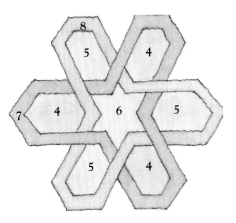

Plan dimensions: 12' x 12'

FORMAL RECTANGLE

Herbs

1 Germander (*Teucrium chamaedrys*)
2 Lavender, dwarf (*Lavandula angustifolia* 'Hidcote')
3 Sage, purple (*Salvia officinalis* 'Purpurascens')
4 Betony, woolly (*Stachys byzantina*)
5 Clove pinks (*Dianthus caryophyllus*)
6 Chamomile (*Chamaemelum nobile*)
7 Orris root, variegated (*Iris* 'Pallida Variegata')

Nonherb

8 Boxwood, dwarf (*Buxus sempervirens* 'Suffruticosa')

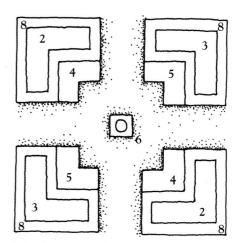

Plan dimensions: 20' x 20'

Alternate patterns

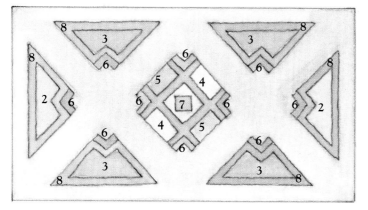

Plan dimensions: 20' x 40'

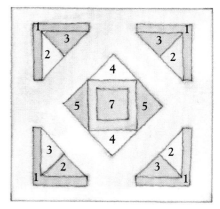

Plan dimensions: 20' x 20'

FORMAL CIRCLE

Herbs

1 Sage, tricolor (*Salvia officinalis* 'Tricolor')
2 Sage, purple (*Salvia officinalis* 'Purpurascens')
3 Sage, variegated (*Salvia officinalis* 'Icterina')
4 Thyme, silver (*Thymus vulgaris* 'Argenteus')
5 Thyme, lemon (*Thymus* × *citriodorus*)
6 Thyme, common (*Thymus vulgaris*)
7 Chamomile (*Chamaemelum nobile*)

Nonherb

8 Boxwood, dwarf (*Buxus sempervirens* 'Suffruticosa')

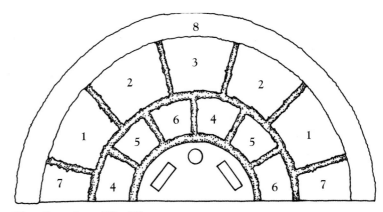

Plan dimensions: 25' x 13'

Alternate patterns

Plan dimensions: 25' x 10'

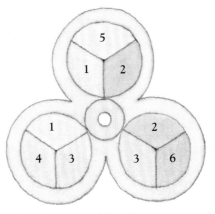

Plan dimensions: 14' x 13'

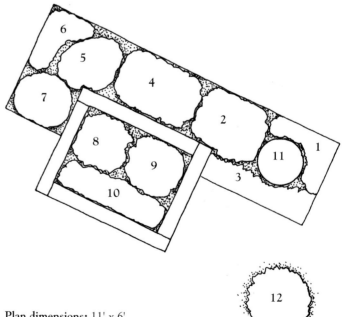

KITCHEN GARDEN

1 Parsley (*Petroselenium crispum*)
2 Basil (*Ocimum basilicum*)
3 Chives (*Allium schoenoprasum*)
4 Sage (*Salvia officinalis*)
5 Oregano (*Origanum vulgare*)
6 Tarragon (*Artemisia dracunculus*)
7 Marjoram (*Origanum majorana*)
8 Winter savory (*Satureja montana*)
9 Rosemary (*Rosmarinus officinalis*)
10 Lemon thyme (*Thymus* × *citriodorus*) and
common thyme (*Thymus vulgaris*)
11 Spearmint (*Mentha spicata*)
12 Bay (*Laurus nobilis*)

Plan dimensions: 11' x 6'
(not including bay tree)

MIXED GARDEN WITH HERBS

Herbs

1. Rue (*Ruta graveolens*)
2. Purple coneflower (*Echinacea purpurea*)
3. Lavender, English (*Lavandula angustifolia*)
4. Feverfew, golden (*Chrysanthemum parthenium* 'Aureum')
5. Orris root (*Iris pallida*)
6. Germander (*Teucrium chamaedrys*)
7. Oregano, golden (*Origanum vulgare* 'Aureum')
8. Catmint (*Nepeta* x *faassenii*)
9. Betony, woolly (*Stachys byzantina*)
10. Cottage pink (*Dianthus plumarius*)
11. Thyme, silver (*Thymus vulgaris* 'Argenteus')
12. Thyme, lemon (*Thymus* x *citriodorus*)
13. Hyssop (*Hyssopus officinalis*)
14. Anise hyssop (*Agastache foeniculum*)
15. Tansy (*Tanacetum vulgare*)
16. Fennel, bronze (*Foeniculum vulgare purpureum*)
17. Wormwood (*Artemisia absinthium*)
18. Sage, purple (*Salvia officinalis* 'Purpurascens')
19. Rose, Apothecary (*Rosa gallica officinalis*)
20. Rose, Variegated Apothecary (*Rosa gallica versicolor*)

Nonherbs

21. Coral bells (*Heuchera sanguinea*)
22. Peony (*Paeonia*) 'Festiva Maxima'
23. Daylily (*Hemerocallis*) 'Stella de Oro'
24. Daylily (*Hemerocallis*) 'Catherine Woodbery'
25. *Sedum* 'Autumn Joy'
26. Lady's mantle (*Alchemilla mollis*)
27. Coneflower (*Rudbeckia fulgida sullivantii* 'Goldsturm')
28. *Spiraea* x *bumalda* 'Anthony Waterer'
29. *Spiraea* x *bumalda* 'Limemound'
30. Rose (*Rosa*) 'The Fairy' or 'Iceberg' (trained as standard)
31. Boxwood, dwarf (*Buxus sempervirens* 'Suffruticosa')

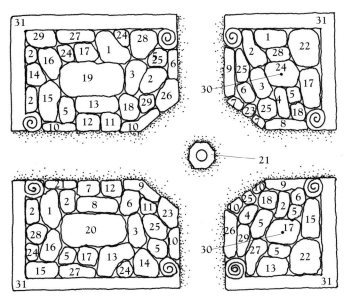

Plan dimensions: 35' x 29'

THE BASICS OF GROWING HERBS

Over centuries of use, herbs have accumulated a body of lore that includes some highly unusual directions for culture. But in contrast to such fanciful advice from antiquity, these plants — though diverse — are among the easiest to grow without any special attention. Anyone who can raise annuals, vegetables, or the easier perennials can succeed with herbs of all kinds. In these pages you'll learn the fundamentals of growing herbs in the garden, in containers, and indoors, as well as how to raise new plants.

Many herbs grow with no special attention to care, but those grown as vegetable crops will respond to cosseting, as this lush stand of French sorrel proves.

25

GARDEN CULTURE

Despite the obvious diversity among the various herb plants, some basic cultivation principles still apply. For specifics on each herb, be sure to consult the encyclopedia beginning on page 33.

PLANTING SITE. Although most herbs prefer a sunny site, some will thrive in shade. What's most important is to choose herbs that will prosper in the conditions offered by the site — or to modify the site to accommodate the herbs you want.

To get off to the best start, try to avoid areas infiltrated by roots of trees and shrubs. With such hidden competition, the herbs may fall far short of your expectations. If possible, choose a sheltered spot not routinely buffeted by strong winds.

Any herb noted as sun loving will require sunlight for at least 6 hours a day under average conditions. Where the sky is often overcast, sunlight needs to reach plants throughout the day. But where summer sun is relentlessly hot, many of these same plants will benefit from a bit of high shade or filtered light during the hottest hours.

SOIL. Despite differing soil preferences among herbs, it's safe to say that most require — and all prefer — well-drained soil. But before you can consider modifying your soil, you need to determine the kind of soil you have and its drainage characteristics. Two tests are outlined at right.

Moisture-retentive clay soils are gluelike when wet but as hard as concrete when dry. Such soils are dense (often called "heavy") because they consist of tiny, flattened mineral particles that pack together almost like cards in a deck. Because of the density, there's little space between particles for water to enter. Thus, water penetrates only very slowly, resulting in poorly drained soil.

Sandy soils, on the other hand, are so porous that water flows through them as through a colander; when dry, they're dusty. Sandy soils are composed of relatively large, irregularly rounded particles that fit together like beans in a jar; spaces between particles let water and air pass freely.

Fortunately, most garden soils fall somewhere between the two. The "ideal" loam soil of gardeners is a mixture of particles, with the important addition of organic matter. The key to improving soil structure, organic matter modifies the drainage excesses of most clay and sand soils.

You can "open up" a claylike soil by digging in quantities of organic matter, ideally from 25 to 50 percent of the soil volume; the organic amendments will act as wedges between clay particles and particle aggregates, letting water percolate more rapidly through the dense soil. In sievelike sandy soil, amendments fill in the pore spaces between particles, slowing the passage of water.

Evaluating Your Soil

Good soil and good drainage are essential to successful plant growth. Perform the following tests on your garden soil to determine the type of soil you have and how well it drains.

SOIL TYPES. Moisten the soil, take up a handful, and squeeze it into a ball. Clay soil will feel smooth or even slimy and, if wet enough, may ooze in ribbons through your fingers. When prodded by a finger, it will remain intact. Sandy soil, on the other hand, feels gritty or granular. If you prod it with a finger, it will fall apart readily; it may even fall apart without encouragement.

Soils between clay and sand will fall between those two extremes. An intermediate-type soil will form a pliable ball that will break apart when prodded.

DRAINAGE TEST. In moist soil, dig a hole a foot deep and wide; fill it with water. If the water disappears within several hours, drainage is probably good. Now fill the hole with water again; with good drainage, this water will be gone in no more than 8 hours. If the second filling takes longer than 8 hours to drain, plant just those herbs that need regular moisture; or build raised beds and fill them with an organically amended lighter soil to accommodate plants that prefer some dryness.

If the first filling has not drained within 8 hours, plant only in raised beds or containers.

Among the most popular organic soil amendments are leaf mold, peat moss, ground bark, and various other nitrogen-fortified wood by-products (look for these packaged products in nurseries and garden centers). Homemade compost is available to any gardener with the space and inclination to prepare it. Regional agriculture frequently spins off by-products that can be used to amend soil; apple and grape pomace, rice hulls, and mushroom compost are examples.

Most herbs are not particular about a soil's acidity or alkalinity. Strongly acid soils are typical of high-rainfall areas; especially alkaline soils generally occur in arid regions. To check your soil's reaction, either use a commercial soil test kit, available at many nurseries and garden centers, or have a soil test done professionally (look under "Soil Laboratories" in the Yellow Pages). Or check with your county agricultural extension service. For information on modifying acidity or alkalinity, consult your county extension agent.

PREPARATION & PLANTING. The best time to prepare soil is at least one month before you want to plant. In cold-winter regions, planting is best done in early spring at the start of the growing season. The time to prepare soil there is in autumn before the ground freezes. Where winter is more mild and you can plant from autumn through winter to early spring, prepare soil from mid- to late summer through autumn.

Using a spading fork, spade, or rotary tiller, work your soil to a depth of 8 to 12 inches. Incorporate organic matter, a scattering of a complete fertilizer (see at right), and any material recommended to adjust acidity or alkalinity. Then rake the soil smooth, breaking up any large lumps. Water the prepared area to settle the soil. Just before you set out plants or sow seeds, rake the soil again to smooth out humps and hollows.

If possible, choose a windless and cloudy or overcast day for planting. This avoids transpiration stress from wind and sun while plant roots are adjusting to their new quarters. Water after planting to establish good contact between roots and soil.

If the plants are small and likely to be attacked by birds or other wildlife, protect them with chicken-wire cages or tents. Permeable plastic floating row covers are good for covering larger areas.

A mulch spread around newly planted herbs not only looks attractive but also helps them establish more rapidly and suppresses germination of weed seeds. Mulch, a layer of organic material spread on the soil's surface, works to retard evaporation and keeps soil cooler than soil directly exposed to the sun. Mulch, then, encourages good root growth, which leads to good growth above ground. In cold-winter regions, delay applying mulch until the soil has lost its winter chill.

Good mulch materials let water penetrate to the soil beneath and remain in place without considerable blowing about by wind. Bark chips and nitrogen-fortified wood by-products are popular choices; pine needles are an excellent homegrown material. Straw is effective and inexpensive, but it will bring a few weed seeds with it.

WATER & FERTILIZER. Annual herb plants need regular watering from planting to harvest.

Perennials will appreciate routine watering during the first year, but once they're established, you can water according to each herb's moisture preference. For best growth, remember to plant together herbs that have similar moisture needs.

Many herbs in the garden require no routine feeding for good growth. Some, indeed, will flourish with no nutrient supplements at all. But you can hardly go wrong if you give plants an annual feeding just when the growing season begins. Choose a complete fertilizer in the 5-10-10 range and scatter it conservatively according to the recommended amounts on the package. Water immediately after you fertilize. As a rule of thumb, figure that the more lush, leafy green herbs are more likely to need nutrient supplements than those with sparser growth and small or gray leaves.

PEST CONTROL. Use particular caution controlling pests in an edible-herb garden. Hand-pick and dispose of beetles and other large pests; hose off smaller predators, such as aphids and spider mites. Control persistent infestations with a solution of insecticidal soap or a pyrethrum-base insecticide, both of which are nontoxic to humans.

CONTAINER CULTURE

Delicate foliage, striking flowers, and varied aromas invite close inspection of herb plantings. What better way to enjoy herbs than to grow them in containers?

You may decide to showcase just one herb in a special pot or planter. Or you can create a small herb garden by combining different plants having the same cultural needs (culinary herbs are naturals for such a planting, which can then be placed within easy picking distance of the kitchen). Even hanging baskets can be used to display herbs with lax stems that will spill gracefully downward.

Where a deck or patio is the only outdoor space, containers create the herb garden. And in

cold-winter regions, containers let you keep tender plants from year to year if you take the plants indoors or into a greenhouse during the winter. Some herbs will grow successfully indoors the year around; for growing tips, see the facing page.

KINDS OF CONTAINERS. You'll find an endless variety of containers, ranging from ordinary terra-cotta pots and wooden planters to elegant urns, bowls, and jars. Whatever you use, be sure it has holes or slits in the bottom so water will flow through easily when soil is moistened.

The earthy simplicity of unglazed terra-cotta clay pots, the most widely available of containers, is a perfect foil for herbs. One type popular for herb growing is the strawberry jar, an urn-shaped pot that has numerous planting pockets at various levels along the sides. Because unglazed clay is porous, moisture can transpire through the clay as well as from the soil surface, thus avoiding waterlogged roots. Note, however, that the soil in these pots will dry more rapidly and need remoistening more often than other types.

Clay pots also come glazed, but glazing eliminates the clay's natural porosity. Also nonporous are plastic containers.

Wooden containers have a mellow appearance, the wood textures and colors harmonizing unobtrusively with the outdoors. Wood is somewhat porous, but less so than unglazed clay. Set wooden containers on cleats or runners to permit drainage and air circulation so wood won't decay.

Paper-pulp pots, generally made of compressed, recycled paper, are lightweight and inexpensive, but they deteriorate in several years' time. Porosity nearly equals that of unglazed clay.

SOIL FOR CONTAINERS. The soil for container plants must be open enough to allow for easy root growth and water penetration but still able to retain moisture. This translates to a medium that's somewhat coarse and that's well supplied with organic matter.

No matter how good your garden soil, it's too dense by itself for container gardening. Instead, opt for packaged potting soil or planter mix, preparations composed specifically for container culture.

Well-lighted window becomes an instant indoor herb garden with the simple addition of plants in containers.

Most of these products contain various mineral and organic ingredients but no actual soil.

To concoct your own planting medium, follow one of the "recipes" below (the second is faster draining than the first):

1. Combine and thoroughly mix 1 part good garden soil (not clay), 1 part river or builder's sand or perlite, and 1 part peat moss or nitrogen-stabilized bark.

2. Combine and thoroughly mix equal parts nitrogen-stabilized bark, peat moss, perlite, and river or builder's sand.

WATERING & FERTILIZING. You can water containers from the top or bottom. For top watering, apply water gently until it begins to flow from the drainage holes. If this water collects in a saucer, discard the water after all has drained through. To water from the bottom, place the container in a saucer of water; capillary action will moisten soil throughout the pot. When the soil's surface appears damp, discard any water remaining in the saucer.

Apply water as soon as soil feels dry ½ inch beneath the surface. During the heat of summer, watering may be a daily routine. Try not to let soil dry to the point that it shrinks from the container sides. If this happens, loosen the soil with a screwdriver and water from the bottom until the surface appears moist and soil again fills out the pot.

Note that regular watering in a freely draining medium rapidly leaches nutrients. Although most herbs don't require fertilizer, container-grown plants will benefit from periodic feedings. During the growing season, use a half-strength dilution of a complete liquid fertilizer twice a month for the leafy, moisture-preferring kinds, monthly for the less thirsty herbs with harder, frequently aromatic leaves. For convenience, you can use pellitized, timed-release fertilizers.

SPECIAL TIPS. The roots of plants in pots are not as insulated from overheating as are plants growing in the garden. Place your containers where they'll be lightly shaded during the heat of the day. Or group containers so plants in the lower pots shade the larger containers.

Indoor Culture

If you're restricted to indoor gardening or you simply want a ready supply of fresh culinary herbs throughout winter, you can accommodate some of the more familiar herbs indoors in windowsill and artificial-light "gardens."

LIGHT. Adequate light is the most critical factor in growing herbs indoors. Most herbs need full sun about 6 hours each day in an average sunny climate. A sunny windowsill, solarium, greenhouse window, or actual greenhouse offers the best-lighted indoor spot, provided the light doesn't push the temperature too high (see below). Where plants receive light from only one side, rotate the containers regularly in the same direction to promote fairly even growth.

Fluorescent lights release you from the constraints of windowsill culture. Two fluorescent tubes in a standard housing with reflector canopy will direct sufficient light onto the plants. Use either special fluorescent tubes designed to simulate sunlight or two ordinary fluorescent tubes, one that emits cool white light and one that emits warm white light. For sun-loving herbs, 40-watt tubes will give good illumination.

Figure that 14 hours of illumination give the equivalent of roughly 6 hours of sunlight. Place plants so their tops are 6 to 12 inches below the lights. Because intensity decreases as fluorescent tubes age, replace the tubes when they've reached about 70 percent of their normal life span.

TEMPERATURE & HUMIDITY. Herbs will grow well indoors in temperatures comfortable for humans. About 70°F/21°C is satisfactory during the day and around 60°F/16°C at night, except for plants depending on natural rather than fluorescent light; then, reduce day and night temperatures by about 5 degrees F during winter.

In many homes, especially during winter, the air is too dry for the plants' liking. A humidity range between 30 and 50 percent is ideal. To enhance humidity, set pots on a bed of gravel in a saucer and keep the gravel bed wet. Evaporating water will raise humidity in the immediate area.

BASIC CARE. Water and fertilize as for container plants (see at left), but continue fertilizer applications beyond the normal outdoor growing period. To combat such pests as aphids and spider mites, spray plants with a solution of insecticidal soap; rinse off several hours later.

PROPAGATION

Among the herbs, you'll find annuals, perennials, shrubs, and trees. Although each can be raised from seed, all but the annuals can be propagated by at least one other method — by taking cuttings, by dividing clumps, or by layering. For the proper propagation methods for each herb, see the encyclopedia beginning on page 33.

SEEDING. You can plant seeds of many herbs in containers for later transplanting to the garden (to get a head start on the growing season, start plants indoors so they'll be sufficiently large to plant outside in early spring). Other herbs are best sown directly in the garden where they are to grow. Both methods are shown below.

For starting seeds, you can use flats, pots, cellpacks, even individual peat pots and pressed peat cubes. Fill any container nearly to its rim with a light potting soil, apply water to firm it, and then scatter seeds over the surface. Cover them with a thin layer of potting soil and gently water. Keep the soil moist until the seeds germinate. When seedlings show a second or third set of true leaves, transplant them to small individual pots where

they'll gain enough size so you can safely plant them in the garden.

Herbs that need to be sown in the soil where they'll grow include the various taprooted herbs and some that have large seeds, such as the nasturtium seeds shown below. Prepare the soil (see pages 26–27). To sow in rows, score a shallow trench, add seeds, and cover with soil; then water. To broadcast seeds, scatter them over prepared soil, lightly rake the soil to establish contact, and water gently.

After seedlings germinate, thin out excess plants so the remaining ones are at the specified best distance from one another.

TAKING CUTTINGS. Perennials and such shrubs as rosemary, sage, and wormwood are easy to start from cuttings.

In spring and summer, take 4- to 6-inch cuttings from the ends of stems; cut just beneath a leaf (or pair of leaves), remove the lowest leaves, and dip the cut end in rooting hormone. Insert the cuttings a third to half their lengths in a pot of light potting mix; then water. Keep the soil moist but not soggy; sprinkle the foliage if it wilts.

After several weeks, test for rooting by tugging gently; cuttings that won't pull out are rooted. Transplant rooted cuttings to small individual pots of the same potting mix; plant in the garden when roots fill the pot.

Seed in containers (at left) or in the ground (at right).

Dip the cutting in rooting hormone before potting.

DIVISION. Perennial, clump-forming herbs, as well as those that form clumps of bulbs or rhizomes, can be dug and separated for increase. Simply dig the clump, shake off soil so you can see the roots, and break the mass into smaller, well-rooted units. With bulbs (like the chives shown below) and rhizomes, you separate a clump into individual plants that have roots and leaves. With perennials, such as woolly betony (see below), you can pull or cut apart a clump into individual plants or into small, well-rooted units consisting of several stems.

LAYERING. Layering, where you take a cutting without actually removing it from the plant, works well with perennials and shrubs that branch close to the ground, such as rosemary (shown below) and the thymes.

Choose a flexible stem close to the ground that's making healthy growth. Dig a shallow trench into which part of the stem can be buried (don't remove it from the plant). Remove those leaves that will be covered by soil and, if the stem is thicker than a knitting needle, make a shallow cut at a leaf node that will be buried. Fill in the trench, covering part of the stem.

After roots are well formed on the buried portion of the stem, sever the connection to the parent plant and move the new, rooted plant to the desired location.

Divide chives (top), betony (bottom) to propagate.

Propagate rosemary by layering.

 N ENCYCLOPEDIC HERBAL

Like the herbals of yore, this modern herbal presents profiles of a variety of herbs and outlines their uses. Here you'll find many of the legends associated with herbs, their historical and present-day applications, and concise descriptions and planting information. The herbs are arranged according to their common names, with the botanical name listed beneath. Many of these herbs will be familiar to anyone who enjoys good food; others will be well known to gardeners who have long appreciated their obvious ornamental qualities; still others will be recognized as old-time (and often effective) home remedies. Whatever your reason for growing herbs, the guidelines presented here will ensure success.

An herbal tapestry showcases feverfew, thyme, and green lavender cotton among violet Veronica officinalis, yellow Coreopsis lanceolata and garlic-relative Allium fistulosum for sculptural accent.

AGRIMONY
(Church steeples, sticklewort)

Agrimonia eupatoria
Rosaceae (Rose family)
Perennial; hardy to 0°F/–18°C

In the days when most medicine was herbal, agrimony was a kind of "good-for-what-ails-you" plant. In ancient Greece, it was believed to have had a positive effect on liver complaints. In later European experience, agrimony was used to treat wounds and various skin disorders, relieve certain fevers, alleviate coughs, and even extract splinters and thorns from the flesh.

The name agrimony is thought to be derived from a Greek word referring to plants that would heal eye troubles; *eupatoria* commemorates King Mithridates IV Eupator of Pontus (in present-day Turkey), who was known as a practitioner of herbal medicine.

Nowadays, agrimony is rarely grown for its medicinal qualities, though in some rural areas an infusion of agrimony may find use as a "spring tonic," cough suppressant, or throat balm. The plant produces a good yellow dye — light yellow from summer-harvested plants, darker yellow when plants are picked in autumn.

DESCRIPTION. A single stem of agrimony looks wispy and insubstantial, but an established clump makes a graceful, delicate addition to a planting of herbs. From a clump of creeping rhizomes, generally unbranched stems rise to an eventual 2 to 4 feet (depending on culture) when blossoming occurs in midsummer.

Each pinnate leaf consists of a leafstalk and opposite leaflets, the overall leaves largest (to 8 inches long) at the base of stems and declining in size toward the tips. Each leaflet is oblong with a toothed margin, green on its upper surface but gray to white beneath, and showing a rough or quilted texture reminiscent of many mints.

The small, five-petaled flowers, appearing in elongated spikes at the ends of stems, resemble yellow blackberry blossoms. The seed capsules that follow are covered with bristly hairs that stick to clothing, responsible for the plant's folk name, cockleburr.

CULTURE. Agrimony is an undemanding plant. In its native territory — from the British Isles south to North Africa and eastward to western Asia — it's a common plant along roadways and ground abandoned from cultivation. You can even find it naturalized along roads in eastern North America.

For good growth, give agrimony well-drained, reasonably fertile soil in a spot that receives full sun (or dappled sunlight in hot-summer regions). Set out divisions in early spring or early autumn. Or start seeds in pots; then set out young plants in the garden.

HARVEST & USES. Pick stems from early to late summer and hang them upside down to dry. From the entire plant — leaves, stems, and flowers — you can make a pleasant tea that has an odor reminiscent of apricots. Dried agrimony can also lend its scent to potpourri and sachet.

ANGELICA
(Garden angelica)

Angelica archangelica
Umbelliferae (Carrot family)
Biennial; hardy to –30°F/–34°C

Angelica, native to northern Europe and western Asia, was common in European herbal practice during the Middle Ages. As its name suggests, many of its associations were with the Christian religion; as the "root of the Holy Ghost," it was used not only against plague but also against a wide range of other maladies. Benedictine monks found perhaps the best use of the plant, as a flavoring in the liqueur that bears their name.

In our time, angelica is best known as an edible plant. All parts are aromatic and flavorful and are used both fresh and dried.

DESCRIPTION. Angelica is an impressive plant, good for garden ornament as well as herbal uses. The foliage resembles celery, greatly enlarged: thick, lettuce green leafstalks bear numerous lance-shaped leaflets with distinctly serrated edges.

Because angelica is a biennial, or sometimes a short-lived perennial, it remains a clump of foliage for its first (and often second) year in the garden. When it flowers, it sends up a thick, hollow stem to 6 feet crowned with a branching spray of flower umbels, each of which looks like a burst of fireworks. Individual blossoms are greenish yellow and insignificant, but the display is very impressive.

CULTURE. Angelica grows best in a good, slightly acid soil that can be kept moist. Dappled sunlight or light shade suits it in hot-summer regions; where summer is cool and moist, it thrives in full sun.

You can easily start plants from seed, but only fresh seed will give good germination. Sow the seeds where you want the plants; or sow in pots and set out plants the following spring. Angelica is taprooted, so only small plants transplant easily.

Normally, the plant will die after flowering and setting seed; new plants will germinate readily from scattered seed if you don't harvest the crop. To prolong life for a few years, cut out the flowering stem after it has formed. This also encourages the plant to make new shoots from the base; these can be detached later and rooted to become new plants.

HARVEST & USES. Leaves, stems, and roots can all be used fresh. The leaves are good in salads; either leaves or leafstalks can be stewed with acidic fruits to add sweetness. Leafstalks may be cooked and eaten like celery; leafstalks and flower stems can also be candied and used as a garnish on pastries.

Pick fresh leaves and leafstalks up to midsummer. You also can use the fresh root as you would celery root; dig, clean, and peel the roots of plants a year old.

Dried or fresh leaves can be steeped in water for tea. Dried leaves and roots are potential potpourri ingredients. The chief use of the plant's seeds is commercial — as flavoring not only for Benedictine but also for Chartreuse and vermouth.

ANISE
(Aniseed)

Pimpinella anisum
Umbelliferae (Carrot family)
Annual

The culture of anise traces back to ancient Egypt, Greece, and Rome. With the Roman conquests, anise worked its way up the European continent to England; centuries later, seeds were taken to the New World by English colonists. Preparations containing anise seeds were claimed to ease bronchial complaints, soothe coughing, and alleviate digestive upset.

DESCRIPTION. Anise closely resembles other herbs in the carrot family. First growth produces a clump of foliage, the stalked leaves bearing rounded to heart-shaped, lobed leaflets. Later, flowering stems elongate, bearing narrow, feathery leaves. Finally, umbrellalike clusters of tiny white flowers appear at stem tops.

Blooming plants reach about 2 feet high, but, compared to its relatives, anise is a bit wispy. Grouped plants give the best garden effect and help support one another.

CULTURE. Anise is a frost-tender annual that grows quickly in warm weather but needs about 4 months to grow and mature a seed crop. Time plantings so freezing weather will have passed by the time seeds germinate.

In coldest regions, sow seeds indoors in small pots; set out young plants in the garden when the danger of frost is past. In warmer regions, sow anise seed directly in prepared soil in the garden; plants are taprooted and do not transplant easily.

Grow anise in reasonably fertile but light, well-drained soil. Choose a location in full sun; water regularly until seeds form.

HARVEST & USES. Because the flavor of anise seeds is licoricelike, they're used to add that distinctive taste to both food (chiefly baked goods) and drink. Pick seed heads when seeds are ripe — generally late summer to early autumn. Hang them upside down in paper bags. Steeped in boiling water, the seeds make a refreshing anise tea; infused in alcohol, they produce Anisette, Pernod, and Ouzo.

During the growing season, use the foliage as a salad garnish for a toned-down version of the flavor in the seeds.

Anise Cookies

¾ cup sugar
2 teaspoons anise seeds
1 cup (½ lb.) butter or margarine, at room temperature
1 large egg
2 tablespoons brandy or 1 tablespoon each lemon juice and water
3 cups all-purpose flour
1 teaspoon baking powder
½ teaspoon each salt and ground cinnamon

Combine sugar and anise seeds; cover and let stand for a day.

In large bowl of an electric mixer, beat butter and ½ cup of the anise sugar until creamy. Beat in egg and brandy. In another bowl, stir together flour, baking powder, salt, and cinnamon; gradually add to butter mixture, blending well. Shape dough into a ball, wrap in plastic wrap, and refrigerate for at least 1 hour or up to 3 days.

Roll dough on a lightly floured surface to a thickness of ⅛ inch. Cut with 2½-inch cookie cutters and place 1 inch apart on lightly greased baking sheets. Sift and discard seeds from remaining anise sugar; sprinkle over cookies. Bake in a 350° oven until golden brown (about 12 minutes). Let cool on racks. Makes about 5 dozen.

ANISE HYSSOP

Agastache foeniculum
Labiatae (Mint family)
Perennial; hardy to 0°F/–18°C

Had anise hyssop grown wild in the rocky, hilly land around the Mediterranean or even in the pastures of northern and central Europe, surely some legend would have accompanied it into today's herbal literature. But no — this is a denizen of the New World, found in north-central North America, where there is no written record to say it was noticed (let alone used) by the indigenous peoples.

But as with other New World herbs, anise hyssop was just waiting to be discovered by immigrants from the Old World who recognized its familiar licoricelike scent and so rescued the plant from wildflower obscurity. The name is only slightly misleading: this is neither an anise nor a hyssop, though its aroma is like the former and its botanical relationship is to the latter.

DESCRIPTION. Well-grown anise hyssop makes a branched, bushy plant to about 3 feet high. Broadly oval, pointed leaves reach 3 inches long, possess a rich green color (they're nearly white underneath), and have serrated margins and the rough, quilted surface found in many mints.

Individual pinkish purple flowers are quite small, but they make a good show midsummer to autumn, when they appear closely grouped in 4-inch upright spikes at the ends of stems. Bees are attracted to the blossoms, which accounts for anise hyssop's value as a honey plant.

CULTURE. Select a sunny spot where soil is well drained and reasonably fertile. Set out young plants after all danger of frost is past. Water routinely throughout the growing season. You can start plants from seed or divide established plants and replant individual rooted sections.

HARVEST & USES. Fresh leaves contribute a sprightly flavor as a garnish in salads and fruit compotes, and either fresh or dried leaves can be the basis for a pleasing anise-flavored tea.

In fact, if you have no need for real anise seed in baking but simply want the flavor for teas and salads, anise hyssop may be the better plant to grow. It's more attractive than anise in the garden, and it's perennial.

BASIL
(Sweet basil)

Ocimum basilicum
Labiatae (Mint family)
Annual

Basil's familiar presence in Italian cuisine belies a colorful history. Ancient Greeks considered the plant unfit for consumption. Medieval superstition associated the plant with scorpions; basil was once suggested as an herb to draw venom from poisonous bites. Many centuries later, the plant was associated with love and devotion. In France, some call it *herbe royale,* and, indeed, the name likely derives from the ancient Greek word for king.

Sweet basil most likely was native to tropical Asia but reached the Middle East in ancient times. In Mediterranean countries, it has become a distinctive culinary herb, flavoring sauces, salads, and meat dishes.

DESCRIPTION. Sweet basil comes in several different forms,

Licorice basil

which vary in flavor, leaf color and texture, and plant size. The basic species is a fast-growing, somewhat bushy plant to 2 feet high, with broadly oval, 1- to 2-inch bright green leaves with smooth surfaces and a somewhat quilted appearance. Small white flowers appear in tiers of green-bracted whorls at stem ends.

The most striking color variants have bronzy purple foliage. The cultivar 'Purpureum' (usually sold as 'Dark Opal') features beet-colored foliage and pinkish lavender flowers. In 'Purple Ruffles', leaves are coarsely and deeply toothed; 'Green Ruffles', with its noticeably quilted leaves, is its green counterpart.

Bush basil (*Ocimum basilicum minimum),* also known as dwarf or Greek basil, makes a dense, rounded plant to 1½ feet high, its oval, somewhat cupped leaves no more than ½ inch long. The tiny-leafed cultivars 'Green Bouquet' and 'Spicy Globe' are even shorter, reaching about 1 foot high.

Several cultivars possess strong scent and flavor overtones of other plants. Among these are plants sold as cinnamon basil, lemon basil, and licorice basil.

CULTURE. Set out plants after all danger of freezing is past. You can sow seeds in place and then thin out, sow seeds in pots and transplant seedlings to the garden, or purchase started plants for immediate planting. Give

basil full sun, regular water, and good, well-drained soil.

Pinch growing plants to promote bushiness and more leaves. When plants show signs of flowering, pinch out flower spikes to prolong the plant's life.

Basil grows quickly, so you can start a second crop a month to 6 weeks after the first batch.

HARVEST & USES. During the warm months, fresh basil leaves are a seasonal luxury to be used in a variety of dishes. You needn't waste a bountiful supply, as basil lends itself to drying, freezing, and preservation in salt. Use it to make flavored vinegar. The best leaves are from younger stems that have not yet borne flowers.

Classic Pesto

2 cups lightly packed fresh basil
1 cup (about 5 oz.) grated Parmesan cheese
½ to ⅔ cup olive oil
1 or 2 cloves garlic (optional)

Whirl basil, Parmesan, ½ cup of the oil, and, if desired, garlic in a blender or food processor until smooth; add more oil, if needed. If made ahead, cover and refrigerate for up to 5 days; freeze for longer storage. Makes about 1½ cups.

BAY
(Laurel, sweet bay)

Laurus nobilis
Lauraceae (Laurel family)
Tree; hardy to about 10°F/–12°C

People everywhere are familiar with the crown of laurel leaves that adorned the head of the victor in ancient Greece. The priestesses at Delphi are said to have consumed laurel leaves before making prophecies, the tree being dedicated to Apollo, the god of prophecy. Today, a vestige of ancient tradition survives in the word "laureate," the recipient of a special honor in art or science.

Nowadays, bay leaves are a typical ingredient in southern Mediterranean dishes.

DESCRIPTION. As you might expect from its historic associations, bay is native to the Mediterranean. There, and in other regions where winters are warm enough for bay to be planted in the ground, you can anticipate an eventual tree to about 40 feet high. Growth is slow to moderate, compact and broadly conical, frequently with several trunks unless you deliberately restrict a plant to one. You can take advantage of this multitrunk habit and plant bay as a high hedge or screen, limiting height with an annual pruning.

New growth is purplish brown, bearing dark green, leathery, broadly lance-shaped leaves to 4 inches long with slightly wavy margins. Flowers are hardly showy: small and greenish yellow, clustered along stems at leaf bases. Berrylike purplish black fruits follow.

Where winter is too cold for planting in the ground, as well as in mild regions, bay makes a splendid container shrub or topiarylike tree. Move it to a greenhouse or well-lighted but cool room when temperatures fall.

You can let a plant follow its natural shape inclination or trim it into a formalized globe, pyramid, or string-of-beads-style topiary. Because the sizable leaves will look mutilated if sheared with hedge clippers, shape with pruning shears so leaves remain uncut.

A similar (and closely related) plant is the California bay (*Umbellularia californica*), also known as California laurel, Oregon myrtle, or pepperwood. Compared with the Mediterranean bay, this tree is "more" in all respects. It can reach great size (to 75 feet high) in the wild, bearing slightly narrower leaves with strong bay aroma and flavor.

In its native western North America, you can grow it as a tree or tall hedge or background screen.

CULTURE. Both bays need fairly well-drained soil but are not particular about fertility. Water young plants regularly to get them established; thereafter, they'll get along with moderate watering and even withstand some drought. In hot-summer regions, plant in partial shade: filtered or dappled sunlight, or light shade during hottest afternoon hours.

HARVEST & USES. The beauty of having a bay tree is being able to pick a leaf whenever you need it in the kitchen. You can pick the leaves in advance, dry them, and store them for future use, but they'll lose some of their pungency with long storage.

Add bay leaves to soups, stews, and other dishes that simmer for a long period of time (remove leaves before serving).

BEE BALM
(Wild bergamot, Oswego tea, monarda)

Monarda species
Labiatae (Mint family)
Perennials; hardy to about
−20°F/−29°C

The botanical name of this herb commemorates Nicholas Monardes, a 16th-century botanist-doctor who wrote the first book (published in 1571) outlining medicinal uses of native North American plants. The common name wild bergamot alludes to the leaves' scent, which approximates that of the Italian bergamot orange grown for its essential oil.

Oswego tea, another name by which this herb is known, acknowledges the leaves' use by Native Americans living in what is now central New York State.

DESCRIPTION. The showier of the two species is *Monarda didyma*, commonly called "wild bergamot" or "Oswego tea." It's a popular component of perennial borders, grown for its colorful summer blossoms that attract hummingbirds and butterflies.

Each plant forms a spreading, shallow-rooted, somewhat invasive clump. Stems rise from the ground to 2½ to 4 feet high (depending on the individual named selection), well foliaged in 6-inch lance-shaped leaves. Tubular, two-lipped flowers (resembling honeysuckle blossoms) appear in one or two whorled clusters atop each stem. Popular named selections include plants with red, pink, violet, or white blossoms.

Monarda fistulosa is a more gaunt, leggy plant of the same size and habit as M. *didyma*, bearing slightly smaller whorls of lavender to pink flowers. Some growers claim the bergamot scent is more highly developed in this species. Certainly, its leaves are more resistant to mildew.

CULTURE. The bee balms grow best in a moist, organically enriched soil, in full sun to slight or dappled shade; in hot-summer regions, a bit of shade is necessary. Given ample water, bee balm will grow lushly and rapidly. (Plants will endure some dryness, but growth will be less robust, and powdery mildew may disfigure the foliage.)

Divide clumps every 2 or 3 years in early spring; replant in new or rejuvenated soil.

HARVEST & USES. For drying, pick leaves during spring and summer — after they've matured but before they start to age and yellow. Pick flowers as they open.

Fresh or dried leaves make a pleasant tea; fresh leaves add a touch of the bergamot flavor to iced drinks and salads. Fresh flowers make colorful accents in salads and beverages. Dried leaves and flowers are good potpourri ingredients.

BETONY

Stachys officinalis, S. byzantina
Labiatae (Mint family)
Perennials; hardy to
−30°F/−34°C

The two betonies, wood betony (*Stachys officinalis*) and woolly betony (*S. byzantina*), are poles apart in appearance and history. Herbalists from ancient Greece through the Middle Ages were effusive in their praise of wood betony, sometimes called "bishopswort." You were sure to find it cultivated in medieval physic gardens, where it was maintained for its presumed efficacy against a range of maladies, including jaundice, palsy, convulsions, gout, consumption, bruises, and bleeding wounds.

In addition, betony was once used as a yellow dye and, because the dried and powdered leaves can cause sneezing, was included in some formulas for snuff. But today, the best that can be said for it is that it makes an acceptable tea.

Woolly betony, often called "lamb's ears," figured not at all in herbal medicine of past centuries. It comes into today's herb gardens on the reputation of its formerly famous relative — and because it's attractive.

DESCRIPTION. Although the two betonies are a study in contrasts, close inspection will reveal how similar the small flowers are.

Wood betony hails from the meadows and woodlands of Europe and adjacent Asia. Each plant is a tight clump of green foliage; the individual leaf, to 5 inches long, is oblong with a heavily veined surface, carried on a leafstalk from the plant's base. Flower stalks appear in midsummer, each rising to 2 to 3 feet and bearing several pairs of nearly stalkless leaves along their lengths; a dense spike of purplish red flowers tops each stem.

Woolly betony comes from Turkey and Iran, where it's accustomed to drier conditions. Spreading, dense clumps consist of narrow, oval gray-green leaves so heavily felted with white wool that they appear to be gray-white. These thick leaves reach 4 to 6 inches long, forming a solid cover of foliage from creeping stems that root as they spread. Plants present a fairly even height of about 8 inches until early summer, when furry flower stalks with smaller leaves rise to 18 inches to present tiered whorls of small, purplish pink

Wood betony

flowers. 'Silver Carpet' is a totally flowerless selection.

CULTURE. Both betonies grow in sun to light shade, though wood betony is more shade tolerant while woolly betony will need full sun in cool-summer regions. Give wood betony average soil enriched with organic matter and water it routinely.

Woolly betony will grow under those conditions, as well as in fast-draining, poor soil with just moderate moisture; after it flowers, cut out the spent flower stalks to offset seed formation, which can provide numerous volunteer plants. When plantings become patchy after several years, dig and divide clumps, replanting well-rooted divisions.

HARVEST & USES. Wood betony can be enjoyed as a tea substitute; brew the beverage from the dried leaves. Woolly betony, on the other hand, is an ornamental component of the herb garden, with no use beyond that to delight the eye.

BORAGE

Borago officinalis
Boraginaceae (Borage family)
Annual

Proclaimed by Roman authors to be the nepenthe of Homer — which, steeped in wine, caused the drinker to forget sorrow — borage has claim to an ancient and illustrious history. The noted herbalist Gerard affirmed the power of borage infused in wine to promote cheer and drive away sadness (no accounts commented on the part the wine may have played). Later writers praised borage's virtues in treating consumption, fevers, jaundice, respiratory complaints, and sore throats.

In times past, borage was a common cooked vegetable, used much like spinach, as well as a constituent of salads and an additive to beverages. These uses persist to this day.

DESCRIPTION. Reaching 2 to even 3 feet high in good soil, borage makes an attractive branching, rounded plant with broadly oval, 4- to 6-inch grayed green leaves with a rough-textured surface; all leaves and stems are covered in bristly white hairs. Every stem terminates in a complex cluster of small, pendant buds that have a silvery sparkle from the ubiquitous white hairs.

From these buds emerge star-shaped blossoms of a particularly clear blue, from sky bright to a darker, violet-tinted shade. Borage will attract bees, needed to pollinate the flowers.

CULTURE. Although borage is an annual, once you have it you're not likely to be without it unless you rigorously weed out volunteer seedlings. Plants are taprooted, so the best way to start them is to sow seeds in place after frost danger is past.

Although plants tolerate poor soil, you'll get the best-looking display in well-drained soil of average to reasonably good fertility. Borage grows in full sun to filtered sunlight or partial shade; plants need only moderate amounts of water.

HARVEST & USES. The leaves, rich in calcium and potassium, taste something like cucumber and can be picked young and cooked as you would spinach. Fresh, uncooked leaves make an interesting garnish in salads and sandwiches and a sprightly additive to iced drinks.

The lovely fresh flowers are attractive decorations for salads and desserts; along with violets, they're favorite flowers for sugaring to decorate fancy desserts. Dried, they add a touch of color to potpourris.

BURNET
(Salad burnet, small burnet)

Poterium sanguisorba (formerly *Sanguisorba minor*)
Rosaceae (Rose family)
Perennial; hardy to –30°F/–34°C

Although to salad burnet were ascribed various general powers, such as the "ability to defend the heart against noisome vapours" (Gerard), the Latin roots of the specific name *sanguisorba* testify to this plant's best-documented medical use: as an astringent to stop the flow of blood in wounds. To do this, the plant was variously boiled down to produce an extract, steeped in water to make an infusion, powdered and made into an ointment, or simply mashed to extract the juice.

Somewhere in these processes of making salad burnet into medicine, it was noticed that the flavor was pleasant, resulting in the plant's popularity in salads, soups, simmered dishes, and various cool beverages.

Throughout its extensive native range in Europe and western Asia, salad burnet (and the related great burnet, *Sanguisorba officinalis*) has for centuries been recognized as a fairly good fodder plant for sheep and cattle, especially in winter when other green foods may be scarce.

DESCRIPTION. Clumps of salad burnet are almost lacy in effect. Each leaf, which arises from the plant's base, consists of a long leafstalk with up to 12 opposing pairs of oval, ¾-inch deeply toothed leaflets. Foliage may reach 12 inches high, a clump of leaves spreading to 2 feet. Upright flowering stems rise above the leaves to a height of 2 feet, terminating in a tight cluster of tiny blossoms in green and rosy red. Plants will self-sow prolifically if allowed to go to seed.

Salad burnet makes attractive clumps of delicate foliage for foreground plantings; it can even be used as small-scale ground cover if flowering stems are routinely cut out.

CULTURE. In the wild, salad burnet grows in poor soils that are neutral to slightly alkaline and where moisture is always available. For garden planting, choose well-drained soil in full sun, in a bed that can be watered routinely.

The simplest way to obtain burnet is to raise it from seed. Once you grow it, new plants are assured if you let a few flowering stems go to seed and scatter it. Otherwise, you can divide young clumps in early spring and replant individual segments.

HARVEST & USES. Nowadays, salad burnet is grown just for the tangy, cucumberlike flavor of the leaves. Pick them while they're fairly young for the best flavor and texture. To keep a supply of leaves coming along, cut out flowering stems as they form.

Add leaves of salad burnet to iced drinks for a slightly spicy effect. Chopped leaves make a pleasant contribution to salads, as well as to cheese and butter sauces and cream soups. Use them, too, to make herb butter and flavored vinegar. Infused in boiling water, salad burnet produces a refreshing tea that is mildly diuretic.

CARAWAY

Carum carvi
Umbelliferae (Carrot family)
Biennial; hardy to –30°F/–34°C

Who would guess that unassuming caraway was once a component of love potions — or that its seeds, when placed beneath a child's bed, would protect against witches?

Native to a vast area encompassing Europe, North Africa, and Asia, caraway seeds have been unearthed in Stone-Age Swiss lake dwellings and Egyptian tombs. In ancient Greece, according to Dioscorides, caraway seeds were prescribed for bringing color into the faces of girls with pale complexions. Romans ate the seeds to relieve indigestion. The name comes from the Arabic word for seed.

Beginning in the Middle Ages, written records focus on caraway's culinary uses — its root

a better-flavored substitute for parsnips, according to Parkinson, and its seeds in breads and cakes and as an accompaniment to baked fruits. Even today, caraway seeds and apples are a familiar combination.

Caraway appears often in foods from Scandinavian and Germanic regions, including the German liqueur Kümmel.

DESCRIPTION. Among the various herbs in the carrot family, caraway has the most carrotlike appearance, with its finely divided, nearly lacy leaves.

During its first year in the garden, each plant makes a 1- to 2-foot-high mound of the filigree foliage. In the second spring, flowering stalks elongate to rise above the leaves and bear flat, umbrellalike clusters of tiny, greenish white flowers. The seeds they form ripen in midsummer, and then the plant dies.

CULTURE. Select a sunny spot for caraway, where soil is well drained and where you can water routinely whenever rainfall fails. Plants are taprooted, so seeds are best sown directly in the soil either in autumn (in mild-winter regions) or early spring.

If you want to start seeds in containers, plant in cell-packs, thin to one plant per cell, and set out plants while quite small.

HARVEST & USES. The seeds, the plant's most useful component, should be picked ripe in midsummer and dried. Put

them to use in making pickles and sauerkraut and in flavoring breads (particularly rye bread), cheeses, soups, meat dishes, and salads. The fresh leaves, finely chopped, impart typical caraway flavor to salads and soups. The root can be cooked as you would parsnip.

Caraway Roll

1 large package (8 oz.) cream cheese, at room temperature
⅓ cup whipping cream
3 cups (12 oz.) shredded jack cheese
1 tablespoon caraway seeds
  Seasoned salt
⅓ cup shredded Parmesan cheese

Beat cream cheese and cream until fluffy. Stir in jack cheese and caraway seeds. Season to taste with salt. Spoon onto foil or wax paper that has been sprinkled with Parmesan. Shape into a log, coating outside with cheese (if mixture is too soft to handle, refrigerate briefly and then shape).

Refrigerate log until firm (about 2 hours). Makes about 12 servings.

CATMINT & CATNIP

Nepeta x *faassenii*, *N. cataria*
Labiatae (Mint family)
Perennials; hardy to
−30°F/−34°C

Catmint (*Nepeta* x *faassenii*) is widely grown as an edging plant for perennial beds and herb gardens. It's somewhat attractive to cats, but not nearly so much as its close relative catnip (*N. cataria*), which has a well-earned reputation for sending cats into states of kittenish friskiness. Today, we know that to cats the catnip aroma is an aphrodisiac.

In times past, however, catnip was known for its medicinal qualities. Nervousness, hysteria, and headache were three complaints said to be eased by catnip. It was also used to relieve fevers and pains associated with colic. As a remedy for bruises, Culpepper suggested drinking an infusion of catnip juice and wine.

Before the arrival of true tea from eastern Asia, a tea made of catnip leaves and flowers was consumed as a beverage in Europe. The plant contains vitamin C, and its tea is mildly sedative.

DESCRIPTION. Catmint's gray-green leaves, oval to nearly arrow shaped with a quilted surface, reach 1¼ inches long. Plants are dense, about 1 to 1½ feet high and spreading wider; loose spikes of small clustered blossoms cover the plants in a lavender blue haze over a long flowering period that begins in midspring.

Named selections include 'Snowflake', with white flowers, and 'Six Hills Giant', which forms a rounded plant to 2 to 3 feet high.

Catnip features arrow-shaped, grayish green leaves with coarsely toothed margins and a textured surface similar to catmint, but up to twice the size of catmint's leaves. Tiny, lavender-spotted white flowers appear in tiered whorls at stem ends on a basically upright plant growing to 3 feet high.

The foliage aroma is a magnet to cats, which will rub against, roll on, and even tear up a plant. The selection 'Citriodora' has lemon-scented leaves.

CULTURE. Both catmint and catnip prefer full sun and average, well-drained soil. Give them routine watering. In early spring, just as growth begins, cut out last year's spent stems to make way for new. After the first flush of bloom on catmint, shear back

Catmint

plants to encourage another flowering cycle.

Catmint is a sterile hybrid; to increase a planting, divide an established clump, layer stems, or take cuttings.

Start new plants of catnip from seed or cuttings. An old aphorism notes that cats will ignore catnip plants raised from seed but will be drawn to those set out as rooted plants. Presumably, the bruising of leaves and stems releases the oils that give cats the come-hither. To be on the safe side, it's wise to protect any young plants until they're large enough to withstand a cat's attentions.

HARVEST & USES. Catmint is strictly ornamental — a decorative border plant for any sunny herb garden.

Catnip, however, is potentially useful. You can add a few fresh leaves to a green salad; fresh or dried leaves make a refreshing tea. And, of course, the dried leaves can be stuffed into little cloth packets to make engaging feline toys.

CHAMOMILE

Chamaemelum nobile (formerly Anthemis nobilis), Matricaria recutita

Compositae (Daisy family)

Perennial (*C. nobile*); hardy to 0°F/–18°C; Annual (*M. recutita*)

Peter Rabbit's mother was following old and widespread tradition when she prepared Peter a cup of chamomile tea. From the British Isles to Egypt, chamomile has been held in high esteem over the years as a sedative, tonic, and general cure-all.

Roman, or English, chamomile (*Chamaemelum nobile*) withstands being walked upon or otherwise compressed, releasing a sweet, applelike aroma. The

plant was a favorite of Elizabethans, who fashioned chamomile lawns and benches for sensory delight. The name, in fact, derives from two Greek words that mean ground apple. Today, chamomile is used in the production of the Spanish sherry Manzanilla, which translates as little apple.

DESCRIPTION. The two chamomiles bear similar white-petaled daisy flowers, but they differ in other respects. The perennial Roman chamomile is a low-growing plant that spreads widely, its stems rooting as they extend. Bright green leaves consist of threadlike segments forming a soft-textured foliage mat to 3 inches high. Foliage is scented of apples.

Summer flowers rise on stems to 12 inches, the typical form having white petals surrounding a buttonlike yellow center. 'Flore Pleno' has creamy white, double flowers that show no yellow centers; 'Treneague' produces no flowers at all.

Annual chamomile (*Matricaria recutita*), also called "German chamomile," features the same finely cut, threadlike foliage, but plants are upright and branching, to 2½ feet tall, and the white petals of its 1-inch flowers bend backwards from yellow centers.

CULTURE. Plant Roman chamomile in well-drained soil in sun to partial shade; in hot-

summer regions, plants may be short lived. Water moderately. When plantings become sparse or show bare patches, dig and replant rooted segments in the spring.

German chamomile prefers a fairly light, well-drained soil and full sun. Plants need only moderate watering and tolerate some drought.

HARVEST & USES. Over the years, debate persisted over which chamomile was better for tea made from the dried flowers. Now it appears that both plants possess the same chemical substances that give chamomile tea its effectiveness. Dried blossoms of the German chamomile are sweeter flavored. Dried flowers and leaves of both chamomiles can be used in potpourri.

The Roman chamomile, because of its low and spreading habit, makes an interesting lawn. You also can plant it between stepping stones or use it to create the seat of an herb bench. The flowerless 'Treneague' maintains a fairly even surface with little or no mowing.

Roman chamomile

CHERVIL

Anthriscus cerefolium
Umbelliferae (Carrot family)
Annual

No legends of magical powers surround chervil, unless you count the magic of preparing well-seasoned foods. Chervil's realm has always been the kitchen, where it has been esteemed at least since the Middle Ages.

This herb and its relative, sweet cicely (sometimes referred to as "giant chervil"), have been confused in the past. For information on sweet cicely, see page 91.

DESCRIPTION. The carrot family contains a number of familiar herbs, all built along the same lines. At one end of the scale you have the imposing plants of angelica and fennel; chervil, by comparison, is much more demure. Its finely cut leaves lie between parsley and some ferns in general appearance.

From low foliage mounds, flower stems rise 1 to 2 feet, bearing umbrella-shaped heads of tiny white flowers in summer.

Chervil leaves smell and taste a bit like parsley but with overtones of anise. It's for this subtly tasty foliage that the plant is cultivated; the seeds merely ensure another crop.

CULTURE. Chervil needs a bit of shade (either partial shade or dappled sunlight), average soil, and routine watering. Sow seeds directly in the garden in early spring (in cold-winter regions) or in autumn (where winter is mild); in subsequent years, volunteer seedlings will keep you supplied with new plants.

You also can grow chervil in containers. Plants bolt to flowering when days are long and temperatures high. Cut out flowering stems as they form to keep the plant's energies channeled into leaf production.

HARVEST & USES. Fresh leaves have the most intense flavor. If you want to dry them, do it at a temperature not exceeding 100°F/38°C for maximum flavor retention. Begin picking leaves when plants are about 6 inches high.

Utilize the fresh leaves, chopped, in salads, soups, butter and cheese sauces, and delicately flavored chicken, fish, and egg dishes. Cooking diminishes the flavor, so add chervil close to the end of the dish's prescribed cooking time. Chervil imparts a subtle flavor to white wine vinegar. In combination with chives, parsley, and tarragon, chervil is a traditional component of the French *fines herbes.*

CHICORY

Cichorium intybus
Compositae (Daisy family)
Perennial; hardy to –40°F/–40°C

Chicory is a plant that's been known to civilization for thousands of years. Its name is thought to have originated in ancient Egypt, a claim made all the more likely by the fact that the name is nearly the same in all countries of the Old World. In the third century B.C., Theophrastus made reference to *cichorium* as a plant even then long in use. Roman writings note its consumption in salads and as a simple vegetable.

Herbalists of the Middle Ages and later attributed a number of medicinal values to chicory. Because chicory's blue flowers close around midday, the Doctrine of Signatures deemed the blossoms useful in treating inflamed eyes. Poultices of leaves were used to ease swelling, while boiled chicory was thought to bolster a queasy stomach. Various liver complaints were subject to chicory's curative powers, and a boiled extract of chicory root was known to be a mild laxative.

DESCRIPTION. Although originally found in Europe and western Asia, chicory is now naturalized in the Americas, Australia, New Zealand, and South Africa. Its clear blue blossoms make it a conspicuous and familiar roadside weed, where it flourishes despite a host of seemingly inhospitable conditions.

Before it flowers, chicory is fairly undistinguished: a clump of oblong leaves, sometimes toothed or slightly lobed. But from this dandelionlike mound rise airy, multibranched flowering stems 3 to 5 feet high bearing 1½-inch narrow-petaled daisies of the purest sky blue (occasionally white or pink) from late spring into summer. Flowers open in early morning and close about 5 hours later.

If you let the flowers go to seed, chicory will give you copious volunteer seedlings.

CULTURE. Chicory will grow robustly in good soil with regular garden care, but it also thrives in fairly poor soil with moderate water. Plants are basically taprooted, with a few strong branching roots.

Sow seeds in containers and transplant young plants to the garden after all danger of frost is past. You can also start new plants from root cuttings taken in late winter to early spring.

HARVEST & USES. The root of chicory — dried, roasted, and ground — is sometimes added to coffee to provide a bitterish bite. But chicory's more common use is as a raw or cooked vegetable. Harvest young leaves to use in stir-fry dishes or as salad greens — red-leafed radicchio is simply a chicory grown for its color.

Belgian endive is actually chicory (usually the cultivar 'Witloof') that has been dug in autumn so the tender, edible new growth can be forced in the dark during winter. The shoots (sold as chicons) are used as salad greens or prepared as a cooked vegetable. However, digging the roots, storing them, and blanching new growth to produce shoots is tedious work; it's easier to splurge and buy them in the market.

For an unusual and attractive salad garnish, add chicory blossoms. The dried petals contribute touches of blue to potpourri.

CHIVES

Allium schoenoprasum
Liliaceae (Lily family)
Perennial; hardy to –35°F/–37°C

In nature, chives occur over a vast geographic range, from Asia through the Middle East to Europe and also in North America. The earliest recorded mention of chives is from China some 4,000 years ago.

Unlike their more pungent relative, garlic, to which a number of magical and medicinal qualities were attributed, chives have always been relegated to the kitchen. Credit for bringing their culinary appeal to European cooks may well belong to Marco Polo, who encountered them in Chinese cuisine during his epoch-making travels in the 13th century.

All the many *Allium* species, which, besides chives and garlic, include onions and shallots as well, contain the same chemical compounds that account for the characteristic odor and taste. The strength of the aroma and flavor depends on the concentration of the compounds; mild-mannered chives possess less of the *Allium* essence than their relatives.

DESCRIPTION. If you know chives only in association with sour cream and baked potato, the live plant will come as a pleasant surprise. This is an attractive ornamental, the reedlike, hollow leaves (with oniony flavor) growing in grassy clumps from small

bulbs. Well-grown plants, spared from snipping for kitchen use, may reach 18 inches high.

Slender stems rise above leaves in spring, each bearing a small, bulblike bud that opens into a spherical cluster of small rose-purple flowers resembling heads of clover blossoms. Plants may be evergreen in mild-winter regions but in colder climates will go completely dormant, to regrow in spring.

The plant known as garlic, or Chinese, chives is the closely related *A. tuberosum*. It also forms clumps of grassy foliage from small bulbs, but the mildly garlic-flavored leaves are flat (about ½ inch across) and powdery gray-green, growing to about 12 inches high.

The summer flower stems exceed the foliage height and bear clusters of small white blossoms that have the scent of violets. Foliage dies down in winter. Garlic chives are less hardy than ordinary chives, withstanding temperatures only to about –20°F/–29°C.

CULTURE. Both ordinary chives and garlic chives grow best in a sunny bed in good, fertile soil with regular watering.

For more plants, you can either sow seeds in pots (for later transplant to the garden) or divide crowded clumps. If you fail to remove spent flowers, you'll surely get a crop of volunteer seedlings. To maintain a winter crop indoors, pot up small clumps

in autumn and take them inside to a sunny windowsill.

HARVEST & USES. Regular chives and, to a lesser extent, garlic chives are familiar as garnishes, not just with baked potatoes but also in cheese and egg dishes, salads, and soups. Use the chopped leaves to make a tasty herb butter or cream cheese, following the directions on page 105. For use in cooking rather than as a garnish, you can dry or freeze the leaves.

CLOVE & COTTAGE PINKS

Dianthus species
Caryophyllaceae (Pink family)
Perennials; hardy to −30°F/−34°C

Ancient Greeks and Romans associated pinks with the highest deity in their pantheons: Zeus and Jupiter, respectively. Since then, the showy flowers of various pinks have been put to medicinal and culinary uses, but their primary roles have been symbolic and decorative. Today, pinks furnish herb gardens with their sparkling colors and a delightful, spicy fragrance.

DESCRIPTION. Clove pinks (*Dianthus caryophyllus*) are familiar in today's gardens as border carnations and florists' carnations. Cottage pinks (*D. plumarius*) are available in named selections, a few of which date back several centuries. Allwood pinks are hybrids between cottage pinks and border carnations. Other popular kinds are maiden pinks (*D. deltoides*) and Cheddar pinks (*D. gratianopolitanus*, formerly *D. caesius*).

Clove pinks

All the pinks are similar, differing chiefly in size. Plants form dense mats or mounds of very narrow gray-green to blue-green leaves from which rise needlelike stems, each bearing one to several fragrant flowers. Blossoms are circular in outline and single, semidouble, or double; petals often have fringed margins, and some flowers are marked by decorative colored edges or central "eyes."

All pinks flower from spring into early summer; some will continue through summer or resume flowering when weather cools.

For garden use, the best selections of clove pinks are border carnations, fairly bushy plants with 12- to 14-inch stems bearing 2-inch fragrant double blossoms in white, pink, red, orange, or yellow. Cottage pinks form lower foliage mats from which spring stems 10 to 18 inches high; the 1½-inch flowers include solid colors and those with contrasting markings. Allwood pinks are similar but flower throughout summer.

Maiden and Cheddar pinks are the lowest growing of all, with ground-hugging mats of foliage and masses of small flowers elevated several inches above the plants.

CULTURE. All pinks need well-drained, light soil (even a gritty one), preferably neutral to slightly alkaline. Pinks thrive in regions that have cool to mild summer weather, where they'll grow in full sun. In hot-summer regions, they need a bit of afternoon shade.

Set out young plants in spring (also in late summer to autumn in mild-winter regions) and water them routinely (don't overwater). Where winter temperatures reach −10°F/−23°C or lower, protect plants with a light covering of evergreen boughs.

When individual plants start to decline, replace them with new plants started from cuttings. Take cuttings of new growth that hasn't flowered, either tip cuttings about six nodes in length or heel cuttings of similar length. Root them in a sandy rooting mix or light garden soil.

HARVEST & USES. Flowers are the useful part, for both fragrance and flavor. Dried blossoms contribute their spicy aroma to potpourri. Fresh flowers can be used to make herb vinegar and flavored sugar. You can add petals to salads for a decorative and tasty accent, but first remove the bitter-tasting white petal bases.

COMFREY

Symphytum officinale
Boraginaceae (Borage family)
Perennial; hardy to –30°F/–34°C

Comfrey is pre-eminently a healing herb. Over the years, it has been used to help mend broken bones, heal wounds, and ameliorate bruises.

References as far back as ancient Greece, but especially from the Middle Ages onward, give testimony to its effectiveness. Boiling the roots in water produced a liquid that, taken internally, could heal ulcers and internal bruises; likewise, external wounds, bruises, swellings, and sprains would be helped by the same brew, to a lesser extent by the liquid of leaves boiled in water, or even by direct application of roots to fresh wounds. A hot poultice of mashed leaves would relieve inflammations.

Today, scientific explanations support the folk wisdom of yesteryear. Modern research has shown that all parts of comfrey contain allantoin, a protein that stimulates healing, and the roots are amply supplied with a mucilaginous substance that will, indeed, bind cuts.

In the last century, comfrey was promoted as a plant that could help end starvation. While it's true that the leaves are rich in protein and key minerals and vitamins, modern scientists have uncovered potentially carcinogenic elements as well, thus casting doubt on the internal uses of this impressively endowed plant.

The studies have been challenged, but as long as controversy exists, it's better to err on the side of caution.

DESCRIPTION. Comfrey makes a handsome, bushy, coarse-textured plant to about 3 feet high.

Branching stems growing from a perennial rootstock bear broadly lance-shaped leaves that are distinctly veined and covered with downy hairs. Leaves at the base of a clump may reach 8 inches long, but they become progressively smaller in the upper reaches of the stems. Their normal color is dark green, but leaves of the selection 'Variegatum' are irregularly margined in white.

Pendant clusters of ½-inch bell-shaped blossoms in purple, dull rose, cream, or white decorate plants over a long period from late spring through summer; they're subtle rather than showy.

In virtually frost-free climates, comfrey remains leafy through winter; in other areas, plants die down in autumn and reappear in spring.

CULTURE. Where summer is cool, you can grow comfrey in full sun; in all other climates, plants prefer at least a bit of shade.

Best growth is in a moisture-retentive soil, or at least with plenty of water. Set out plants where you're sure you want them: roots delve deeply, and any piece of root left in the soil after digging will sprout.

HARVEST & USES. Comfrey is best grown strictly for its historical value. However, its purportedly mineral-rich leaves decompose quickly and are used by organic gardeners in making compost and, dug into the soil, as a green manure.

CORIANDER
(Cilantro, Chinese parsley)

Coriandrum sativum
Umbelliferae (Carrot family)
Annual

An ancient and widely grown herb, coriander is referred to in the Bible, in Sanskrit writings, and in Roman records. Although old Chinese belief holds that coriander seeds can confer immortality, the principal use of both seeds and leaves is culinary. Diverse cuisines, from India to North Africa to Europe and to Latin America, employ coriander's distinctive flavors.

DESCRIPTION. Coriander clearly shows its kinship to the other annual herbs in the carrot family: anise, caraway, chervil, and parsley. Each coriander plant grows a central stem to perhaps 18 inches high, ultimately crowned with an umbrella-shaped cluster of tiny, pinkish white flowers. Side branches, with secondary flower clusters, grow from the main stem.

Leaves on the main stem are oval with toothed edges, but those on the branches are more deeply cut to feathery, closer in appearance to the leaves of anise or dill.

CULTURE. An easy and rapid grower, coriander needs a sunny site, routine watering, and good, well-drained soil. Where summer is very hot, give plants a bit of light shade.

Sow seeds directly in the garden where you want the plants; coriander is taprooted and transplants poorly. Because hot days and short nights rush plants to flowering, sow seeds as soon as all danger of frost is past so you'll have the longest possible harvest period.

If you intend to reap entire young plants rather than just a few leaves at a time, you can plant successive crops at 2-week intervals for a continuous harvest until weather turns hot. You can also sow seeds in containers and keep a crop coming along close to the kitchen.

HARVEST & USES. Begin to pick tender young leaves (or entire young plants) when plants have reached about 6 inches high. Use leaves fresh — they lose most of their flavor when dried. To save the seeds, pick the flowering stems after seeds ripen in midsummer and dry them.

Coriander seeds and the fresh leaves (called "cilantro" or "Chinese parsley") are widely used in diverse cuisines. Their flavors differ, however. The seeds are reminiscent of lemon and sage, with a slightly bitter, musty quality. The leaves and stems have a strong, sharp, slightly bitter flavor and a pungent aroma.

Use the seeds to flavor stews, bean dishes, and some pastries. Fresh leaves combine well with fowl and meats in spicy recipes; use them in salsas, salads, and soups as well.

Salsa Cruda

2 *medium-size firm-ripe tomatoes, cored, seeded, and diced*
1 *medium-size onion, diced*
½ *cup lime juice*
¼ *cup chopped fresh cilantro*
  Salt and pepper

In a bowl, mix tomatoes, onion, lime juice, and cilantro. Season to taste with salt and pepper. If made ahead, cover and refrigerate for up to 3 hours; stir before serving. Makes about 2½ cups.

COSTMARY
(Alecost, Bible leaf)

Chrysanthemum balsamita
Compositae (Daisy family)
Perennial; hardy to –20°F/–29°C

This herb's aroma is accurately described by the specific name, *balsamita*. Its common name, costmary, is a compounding of two other words that further describe the plant. From the Latin *costum*, meaning an aromatic Oriental herb, its Asian origin is indicated. From "mary," widespread European association of the plant with the Virgin Mother is acknowledged.

The two other common names could hardly represent more opposing uses. Before hops became the flavoring of choice for English beer and ale, costmary leaves were used instead. And when the plant was transported to Colonial America, costmary leaves were literally pressed into use as bookmarks during church services and daily Bible readings.

In past centuries, costmary was a kitchen garden plant, its leaves used in salads, soups, and stews, and with roasted meats. But the plant was also credited with various remedial properties. In particular, it was believed to have value as a mild laxative, as a cure for congested sinuses, and as a vermifuge for children.

DESCRIPTION. Because of its bold foliage, costmary is useful in the herb garden for texture contrast. Oval, grayish green leaves with toothed margins grow to 7 inches long, making leafy clumps directly from the ground. Stiffly upright, branched flower stems rise to 2 to 4 feet high in summer, bearing ½-inch daisy flowers with white petals and yellow centers. The form *Chrysanthemum balsamita tanacetoides* has flowers that lack petals.

Some gardeners think the flowering stems impart a weedy look to the plants, but this is easily remedied if you cut out the stems so the foliage remains the primary focus. Leaves die down over the winter; a new crop appears in the spring.

CULTURE. The most luxuriant foliage occurs when costmary is planted in good soil in full sun to partial shade and is given regular watering.

If you want to extend your planting, dig a clump in early spring (in cold-winter regions) or autumn (in mild climates), separate it into smaller, rooted pieces, and replant them. After several years, you may want to dig and divide established clumps to curb their spread.

HARVEST & USES. The aroma and rather sharp flavor of the leaves account for costmary's usefulness. Clip fresh young growing tips to use sparingly in salads and soups.

The balsamlike aroma persists after drying, so dried leaves can be employed wherever the scent would be welcome. Use the dried leaves in potpourri, as well as in drawers and closets where the aroma can permeate linens and clothing.

DILL

Anethum graveolens
Umbelliferae (Carrot family)
Annual

Records of dill date back to ancient Egypt — not surprisingly, since the plant comes originally from adjacent southwest Asia. Uses in early Egyptian and Greek civilizations focused on dill's presumed medicinal value; Biblical reference to dill as a tithe indicates the importance of the herb.

In the Middle Ages, dill was used both by magicians in casting spells and by the general populace as a talisman against sorcery. And Culpepper recommends inhaling the vapors of dill boiled in wine as a cure for hiccups.

Today we know that dill does have medicinal value, particularly in soothing stomach discomfort. But gardeners now grow dill for the flavor its seeds and leaves impart to a variety of foods.

DESCRIPTION. Dill's feathery foliage, composed of threadlike segments, immediately recalls that of fennel, a relative; the umbrella-shaped flower heads stamp it as a member of the large and useful carrot family.

Each plant consists of a single hollow stem reaching 3 to 4 feet high at maturity — about 2 months after you sow the seeds. Individual flowers are small and greenish yellow, carried in heads to 6 inches across. Seeds ripen in early autumn.

CULTURE. Choose a location in full sun, where soil is good, and sow dill seeds directly where you want the plants. When seedlings are small, thin plants to about 1½ feet apart. For a prolonged crop, make several successive sowings at 2-week intervals during spring. Give plants routine watering.

Harvest scrupulously in order to avoid volunteer seedlings the next year.

HARVEST & USES. Both leaves and seeds possess the characteristic dill aroma and flavor. Both can be used fresh or dried (the dried leaves are known as dill weed), but the leaves are more flavorful when they're freshly picked.

The seeds' flavor is a bit stronger than that of the leaves, with a sharp and slightly bitter taste reminiscent of caraway.

You can pick leaves as needed during the growing season. To have them available in other months, dry them at temperatures lower than 100°F/38°C or freeze them. Seeds ripen, ready for harvest, several weeks after the plants flower.

Use chopped leaves in salads, dressings and sauces, soups, and egg dishes; with potatoes, various vegetables, fish, poultry, and sour cream; and to make herb butter or cream cheese.

You can use the seeds in many of the same dishes, as well as in herb vinegar and in recipes for bread, apple pie, cabbage, and pickled vegetable preparations.

Some dill pickle recipes stipulate the use of entire flower heads rather than just the seeds.

Dill Dressing

- ½ cup plain yogurt
- 2 tablespoons olive oil or salad oil
- 3 tablespoons chopped fresh dill or 1 tablespoon dill weed
- 2 tablespoons lemon juice
- ½ teaspoon pepper

In a small bowl, mix yogurt, oil, dill, lemon juice, and pepper until blended. Use dressing on cooked green beans, broccoli, and other vegetables. Makes about 1 cup.

ELECAMPANE

Inula helenium
Compositae (Daisy family)
Perennial; hardy to –40°F/–40°C

Lovely elecampane is enveloped by romantic legends. According to one account, this is the plant that Helen of Troy was picking when she was carried off by Paris. Another story asserts that elecampane grew from the tears Helen shed upon her abduction. Since the plant is native to the part of the world that encompasses ancient Greece, it's not difficult to imagine some association with Helen.

From Roman times, roots of elecampane have been accorded medicinal value for a range of problems. In the last century, candied roots were consumed to relieve asthma, bronchitis, and sore throats. Elecampane also figures as an ingredient in absinthe.

DESCRIPTION. It's easy to see why Helen might have been gathering elecampane at just the wrong moment. This handsome plant, strikingly large in size and bold in texture, provides a good contrast to the many smaller, more fine-textured herbs.

Lowest leaves can reach 2 feet long, springing from a clump of rhizomes. Branched flowering stems carry progressively smaller leaves as they rise to around 6 feet. All leaves are broadly ovate and taper to a point; they're rough and sandpapery on upper surfaces, velvety beneath.

Summer flowers are bright yellow daisies that resemble thin-petaled sunflowers; at 3 inches across they're a bit modest floating atop the substantial foliage.

CULTURE. Provide a sunny spot, good soil, and regular moisture. For a handsome study in contrasts, combine elecampane with the equally tall but quintessentially feathery bronze fennel (see page 56).

You can grow elecampane from seed, but it's faster to start with a division from an established clump. It will also grow from root cuttings. To increase a planting, dig and divide established clumps in late summer.

HARVEST & USES. Nowadays, elecampane is grown primarily for its decorative appeal. You can candy the dried root to make an herbal sweet that also serves as a throat lozenge. Dig healthy, 2-year-old clumps in late summer, thoroughly clean the roots, and slice them into rounds for drying; when dry, they have the aroma of violets. Dried flower petals add a dash of yellow to potpourri.

FENNEL

Foeniculum vulgare
Umbelliferae (Carrot family)
Perennial; hardy to –20°F/–29°C

Lovely fennel, native to the Mediterranean, was valued by the ancient Greeks and Romans for both medicinal and culinary purposes. Dispersed throughout a vast empire by the Roman legions, it was recommended for restoring failing eyesight, easing intestinal discomfort, increasing lactation in nursing mothers, and trimming obesity.

As a food, all parts of the plant — roots, leaves, stems, shoots, and seeds — were consumed. Strength and courage were two qualities it was supposed to enhance.

In continental Europe, the spread of fennel was furthered by decree of Charlemagne, who specified its cultivation on the imperial plantations. In addition to its other attributes, fennel was accorded power to ward off evil spirits.

DESCRIPTION. Fennel manages to be both statuesque and delicate at the same time. An established clump will contain numerous vertical stems to 5 to 7 feet high bearing quantities of leaves intricately divided into threadlike segments that give an ostrich-plume effect.

Each stem may branch in its upper reaches, the stem apex and branch ends bearing flat-topped clusters of small yellow flowers. Stems die to the ground in autumn, to be replaced by new growth from the roots early the following spring.

Two variations are noteworthy. Bronze fennel (*Foeniculum vulgare purpureum*) has bronzy purple new growth that lightens to bronze green by midsummer. Florence fennel (*F. v. azoricum*, often listed as *F. v. dulce*) is treated as an annual, grown for its swollen, almost bulblike leaf base, which is harvested for culinary use.

Because it seeds itself prolifically, fennel will quickly become a garden weed unless you harvest the seeds before they scatter; if you don't want a seed crop, remove flower heads before they form seeds.

CULTURE. Fennel looks best when grown in full sun; in fact, the bronze-leafed variant is more intensely colored in sunshine. Sow seeds where you want plants (plants are taprooted); or sow in containers and set out seedlings while they're quite small. Give them well-drained, reasonably good soil.

Fennel is amazingly drought tolerant but grows better with at least moderate watering. When a clump's vigor declines after a number of years, replace it with a new seedling plant.

HARVEST & USES. Fennel leaves and seeds have a pleasant licoricelike flavor. Once you smell the plant, you'll recognize fennel's contribution to certain Italian dishes.

You can pick leaves throughout the growing season for use as garnish in salads, soups, and cooked vegetables; to have leaves available during winter, freeze them. The leaves also make an interesting herb vinegar. Harvest seeds when ripe and use them in sauces, baked goods, and sausages, as well as for brewing a pleasant tea.

Florence fennel is often prepared and cooked in the same way as a root vegetable; it can also be shredded or sliced and used raw in salads and sandwiches. Dig plants for harvest just before they flower.

FEVERFEW

Chrysanthemum parthenium
Compositae (Daisy family)
Perennial; hardy to −30°F/−34°C

The word "feverfew" is a corruption of a Latin word that means essentially the same thing, testimony to the long use of this humble chrysanthemum for medicinal purposes. In times past, it was employed to reduce nervous tension and relieve various pains, particularly those associated with ears, teeth, and joints.

Feverfew also had a reputation for relieving the pain of insect bites, stings, and bruises when applied as a poultice to the affected area. As a bitter tea, it has been consumed as a general tonic.

But perhaps the most noteworthy claim made for feverfew (and one at least 200 years old) is its ability to reduce or relieve headaches, particularly migraines. In recent years, medical research has supported this assertion; many migraine sufferers have found that feverfew reduces the headaches in both intensity and frequency.

DESCRIPTION. Feverfew, in the past called "matricaria," is an old-fashioned garden favorite. Dense foliage clumps consist of lobed, rather feathery bright green leaves with a pungent, peppery aroma. In late spring or summer, leafy stems elongate to 2 to 2½ feet high, bearing large branched clusters of single white daisies less than an inch across.

Named selections offer variations on the basic theme. 'Silver Ball' has double flowers containing mostly white petals; 'Golden Ball' has yellow flower heads that completely lack the white ray petals. For a low-growing, compact plant, there's 'Tom Thumb White Stars'. But the showiest of all the selections is 'Aureum' (often sold as 'Golden Feather'), which has the typical single white flowers backed by bright chartreuse foliage.

CULTURE. A sunny location, well-drained and reasonably good soil, and routine watering will guarantee success with feverfew, though the almost unavoidable volunteer seedlings will persist (even prosper) in conditions far below optimum. Sow seeds where you want plants in the garden; or sow in containers and plant out the young seedlings.

A feverfew in full flower may become top-heavy and need staking; to offset this, pinch back new growth in midspring to induce branching. This also helps keep plants from becoming sparse at their bases.

An individual plant usually remains in good condition for no longer than 2 years, but an ample supply of volunteer seedlings will provide replacements if you let spent flowers form seeds. Transplant them to desired locations in spring. To start new plants from an established planting, you have two options: in spring, you can take cuttings of young stems, or you can divide clumps and replant rooted segments.

HARVEST & USES. Although fresh leaves can be ingested routinely to forestall migraines, their flavor is unappealing and some people suffer oral irritation from chewing the leaves. Migraine sufferers can find feverfew in capsule form.

'Golden Feather' feverfew

FOXGLOVE

Digitalis species
Scrophulariaceae (Figwort family)
Biennial, perennial; hardy to –20°F/–29°C

Although this plant's name may evoke the image of a well-turned-out animal, the word "foxglove" more likely is a misinterpretation of "folkes-glove," a reference to the good folk, or fairies, who dwelt in the woods along with this plant. *Digitalis* comes from the Latin word for thimble, which accurately depicts the individual blossom.

Foxglove came to herbal notice during the Middle Ages, when it was recommended to alleviate a variety of complaints, especially sores and wounds. Then, in the late 18th century, an English physician happened upon a folk remedy for dropsy that he thought was nearly miraculous. Investigating the herbs used in the compound, he concluded that foxglove was the effective agent.

Modern medical research has borne out the efficacy of foxglove in treating accumulations of fluid, especially those associated with the heart. Digitoxin, a glycoside derived from several foxglove species, is now standard in the treatment of certain heart diseases.

DESCRIPTION. The stately foxglove, a classic cottage-garden ornamental and the plant used by the medieval herbalists, is the biennial species *D. purpurea*.

From clumps of large, furry, tongue-shaped leaves rise tall, flowering spikes in spring to early summer. Pendant, thimble-shaped blossoms are arranged on one side of each stem; colors include white, lavender, pink, and purple, all usually spotted with purple in their throats.

Well-grown specimens reach 4 to 6 feet high. Nurseries and seed houses offer several named strains that feature fuller flower spikes, larger individual flowers, and blossoms held nearly horizontally.

Several perennial foxgloves offer plants of the same general appearance but reaching heights of only about 3 feet. The hybrid *D.* x *mertonensis* gives you flowers of an appealing coppery rose color. Yellow foxglove (*D. grandiflora*, hardy to –30°F/–34°C) has pale yellow flowers lightly spotted with brown in their interiors.

CULTURE. All foxgloves are at their best in filtered sun to light

or partial shade, though where summer is cool you can plant in a sunny location. Give plants good soil and regular watering.

To grow the biennial *D. purpurea*, you can either sow seeds in containers and transplant seedlings to the garden later in spring, sow seeds directly where you want plants, or set out nursery-grown plants in autumn or early spring. These plants will spend their first year growing into thrifty clumps; in the second spring to summer, they'll reward you with flowers. If you let flowers go to seed, you'll get a crop of volunteer seedlings.

To raise perennial foxgloves, set out plants in early spring. When they become crowded, divide clumps in early spring. To coax a second flower display, cut out spent spikes after the first flowering.

HARVEST & USES. Despite its medical usefulness, grow this plant purely for decoration. Ingestion of the plant can be fatal.

GARLIC

Allium sativum
Liliaceae (Lily family)
Perennial (bulb) grown as an annual

Garlic, a popular flavoring throughout the world, has a truly impressive history of medicinal use. From ancient times, when Egyptian pyramid builders ate it for stamina, to present-day accounts of its role in the diets of some extremely aged people, garlic has been valued as a strengthening agent. Its antiseptic properties, from healing wounds to acting as an inhibitor of diseases, have been proven. And research into garlic's value continues today.

DESCRIPTION. While a bed of garlic plants may not be a thing of beauty, clumps of the plants can be attractively worked into an overall herb planting.

Garlic is a perennial that grows from a bulb; plants reach 2 to 3 feet high during spring and early summer, only to die back to the bulb after flowering. Leaves are narrow and flat, green to

Rocambole

gray-green, growing generally upright but tending to bend over toward their tips; they sheathe the flower stalk, which produces a small cluster of white flowers at its apex.

Rocambole (*Allium sativum ophioscorodon*), or serpent garlic, offers a decorative twist — literally — to the basic pattern: the flower stalk coils into a loop just beneath the cluster of blossoms. Elephant garlic (*A. ampeloprasum*) is larger in all its parts than regular garlic. The plant easily reaches 3 feet in height and produces fist-size bulbs with a milder garlic flavor.

CULTURE. The cluster of garlic cloves (actually individual bulblets grouped together into a head and covered by a paperlike membrane) you buy at the grocery store is the result of one season's growth under optimum conditions. Each clove, or bulb, is capable of producing its own head of cloves in a season's time.

To start a garlic plant, buy a head of garlic, break it apart, and plant the cloves, base down, in good, well-drained soil where they'll get full sun and regular water during spring and summer. Where winter is relatively mild, you can plant in autumn for a harvest early the following summer. In cold-winter areas, plant in early spring.

HARVEST & USES. Garlic is ready for harvest when leaves turn yellow and fall over (to hasten ripening, bend plants to the

ground when leaves begin to yellow). Dig carefully so bulbs remain intact, remove as much soil as possible, and let the bulbs dry in a well-ventilated place. Remove tops and roots; or leave the dry leaves intact and braid them into decorative ropes.

Although many of garlic's reputed medicinal values are being supported by modern research, the plant's chief usefulness is in cooking, where it flavors an array of dishes in cuisines from around the world. To make a jelly with garlic, see page 106.

Foolproof Garlic Dressing

½ cup each olive oil and seasoned rice vinegar
1 clove garlic, pressed
¼ teaspoon salt

Combine oil, vinegar, garlic, and salt in a jar with a tight-fitting lid. Cover and shake vigorously. (For a creamy dressing, combine ingredients in a blender and whirl until well combined; transfer to a jar.) Let stand for several hours; shake before using. Makes about 1 cup.

GERMANDER
(Wall germander)

Teucrium chamaedrys
Labiatae (Mint family)
Perennial; hardy to –10°F/–23°C

Humble germander once was credited with a number of curative powers. Yet today, you'll not find the plant used in any of its former capacities, unless you can get a vintner to reveal the company's formula for vermouth.

As early as the first century A.D., the Greek physician Dioscorides recommended an extraction of germander mixed with honey as relief for coughs and certain bronchial distresses. Roughly 1,500 years later, Culpepper proclaimed germander's efficacy in treating snake bites, persistent headaches, convulsions, fever and chills, and melancholy.

But the most prominent testimonial to germander's curative powers came in the 16th century from Charles V, Holy Roman Emperor and later King of Spain, whose gout was cured by prolonged ingestion of germander extract.

The specific name *chamaedrys* combines Latin words that mean ground and oak, a good description of the plant's low, spreading growth habit and leaves that recall those of certain evergreen oaks.

DESCRIPTION. Germander, with its glossy, dark green leaves, always manages to appear neat and healthy. Individual leaves are nearly an inch long, oval with toothed edges, and are placed close together on stems, producing a fairly dense foliage mass.

Plants consist of spreading stems to about 2 feet, with branches that reach about 12 inches high; in summer, spikes of ¼-inch reddish purple flowers appear at the ends of branches. With a bit of searching, you may locate a white-flowered form; more commonly available is *Teucrium chamaedrys* 'Prostratum', which may grow to a spread of 3 feet but to a height of just 6 inches.

Bush germander (*T. fruticans*) is a good-looking shrub suitable for herb gardens where winter temperatures won't fall below 10°F/–12°C. Its stems and 1¼-inch-long leaves are silvery gray, the plant becoming a dense, interlaced mound to 4 to 8 feet high and wide.

CULTURE. Trouble-free germander thrives even where soil is poor and water infrequent. In fact, too much water can be its undoing. For best results, plant in full sun in well-drained, average soil and water moderately.

Although you can start germander from seed (which may be a bit slow to germinate), it's far simpler to set out young plants. It grows easily from cuttings taken in spring and early summer. The stems also root here and there where they touch the soil, so you can detach rooted pieces to start new plants.

Germander makes a pleasant informal patch at the foreground of an herb garden, but its more traditional use is as a small hedge plant, a stand-in for boxwood in formal planting schemes. Trim plants once or twice a year to enforce orderliness.

HARVEST & USES. Today's herb gardens contain germander for its historical associations and good appearance.

HOREHOUND
(White horehound)

Marrubium vulgare
Labiatae (Mint family)
Perennial; hardy to –30°F/
–34°C

Medicinal use of horehound can be traced to ancient Egypt, where it was known to priests by several names, including seed of Horus. Our familiar name for it, though, derives not from the Egyptian but from Old English words that meant downy plant.

However, the Latin name, *Marrubium*, does have an Egyptian connection: it stems from the Hebrew word *marrob*, which means bitter. Reputedly, this was one of the bitter herbs to be eaten during the Passover feast celebrating the deliverance of the Hebrews from slavery in Egypt.

Over the years, horehound has been called upon to address complaints as diverse as tuberculosis and bites of mad dogs. But in times past, just as now, the plant's greatest effectiveness has been in the realm of relieving coughs and certain bronchial irritations. The usual vehicles were horehound candies and syrups. The candy lozenges soothed irritated throats; the syrups brought up mucus from the respiratory tract.

Horehound tea has been thought to have tonic properties and to have some beneficial effect on the common cold. In fact, the leaves do contain some vitamin C.

DESCRIPTION. Even if you don't know horehound by name, you may have encountered it as a rather attractive weed. Native to the Mediterranean region and adjacent western Asia, it has become a world traveler, appearing "wild" throughout Europe and North and South America.

A capsule description would say "wrinkled and woolly." Individual leaves are gray-green and egg shaped to nearly round, and so heavily veined as to appear quilted. A woolly white fuzz covers the aromatic leaves and the square stems typical of the mint family.

Horehound forms a branching, shrubby plant to 1 to 3 feet tall, its tiny white flowers coming in whorls where leaves join stems. Plants flower in their second year from seed.

CULTURE. Poor soil, little water, full sun: what could be simpler? Good drainage is the most important point; with that assured, horehound will also grow in better than poor soil and with more frequent applications of water.

Sow seeds in spring in containers; then transplant seedlings to the garden. Or sow seeds directly outdoors and thin seedlings to the desired number.

After you've established horehound in your garden, you'll get an annual crop of volunteer seedlings (to the point of being a nuisance) if you let flowers go to

seed. You can also start new plants from cuttings in late spring and summer or divide clumps in early spring.

HARVEST & USES. Horehound tea is made with fresh leaves (dried leaves lose their flavor) and boiling water. Horehound candy, to be used as cough lozenges, involves boiling fresh leaves to obtain an extract, straining the liquid and letting it cool, and then adding sugar and boiling again until it becomes syrupy. Pour the syrup onto a shallow pan to cool; then cut into pieces.

HORSERADISH

Armoracia rusticana
Cruciferae (Mustard family)
Perennial; hardy to –20°F/–29°C

Horseradish and roast beef seem so inextricably linked that it's hard to imagine there was a time when the English didn't consider the plant edible. Credit for bringing it to the table goes to the Germans and Danes. But throughout Europe in the Middle Ages, horseradish leaves and roots were put to a variety of medicinal uses: as a diuretic, as a digestive aid with rich foods, as a treatment for sore throats and scurvy, and even as a lotion to remove freckles!

DESCRIPTION. The garden appearance of horseradish is like that of its flavor: assertive. A plant is a clump of broadly lance-shaped leaves to 1½ feet long, each leaf carried at the end of a leafstalk that springs directly from the ground; leaves are heavily veined and have toothed margins. The white flowers, in contrast, are almost inconsequential, carried above the leaves in airy sprays.

The roots, which furnish the raw material for the famous sinus-clearing sauce, are long and rope-like. Pieces of root left in the soil after digging will sprout new plants, making horseradish difficult to eradicate once you have it.

CULTURE. For best growth and root development, give horseradish a sunny location and good, well-dug soil. Water regularly throughout the growing season.

To introduce horseradish into your garden, buy a small plant from a nursery. Or obtain root cuttings from an established clump in a friend's garden; using sections of finger-thick roots 4 to 6 inches long, set them vertically into the soil, slender end down, with the top of the cutting about 2 inches beneath the surface. Space plants at least 12 inches apart.

The plant can also be grown in large containers. The oak half-barrels sold at many nurseries offer plenty of room for root development. From such a container, you can easily harvest root pieces as needed; or harvest the entire plant and then replant with new root cuttings.

HARVEST & USES. If you have an established horseradish clump, you can harvest fresh roots just by digging soil away and cutting what you need. To harvest an entire plant, dig in autumn as late as possible before soil freezes, since major root growth occurs in late summer and autumn.

Fresh roots offer the best flavor and pungency. To maintain their freshness for up to 3 months, slice or grate them and refrigerate.

Fresh Horseradish

1 horseradish root (about 1 lb.)
1 cup distilled white vinegar
1 teaspoon salt
½ teaspoon sugar
1 small turnip, peeled and cubed

Peel horseradish root, cutting away dark spots. Cut into cubes (you should have about 3 cups).

Place vinegar, salt, and sugar in a blender. Add about a third each of the horseradish and turnip. Whirl until smooth, scraping down container sides occasionally. Gradually add remaining horseradish and turnip, whirling until vegetables are uniformly grated. Makes about 3 cups.

HYSSOP

Hyssopus officinalis
Labiatae (Mint family)
Perennial; hardy to –30°F/–34°C

This plant's name is from the Greek *hussopos*, which, in turn, was taken from the Hebrew *esob*, meaning holy herb. Here, then, is a plant that attracted early notice. (A plant called "hyssop" is mentioned in the Old Testament, but it more likely is another mint family member — perhaps marjoram or savory — rather than the herb we know by that name today.)

As a medicinal herb, hyssop was used as a tea or poultice to treat a variety of ailments, including bronchial problems, sore throats, and flagging appetites. It was also accorded some sedative value, and the crushed leaves were reputed to promote rapid healing of cuts. Hyssop tea is an old folk remedy for rheumatism.

Culinary applications — chiefly in salads, soups, and stews — apparently were a matter of taste. A little of the hyssop flavor might be palatable in food, but in excess the taste could be unpleasant.

The highly aromatic quality of hyssop made it one of the preferred strewing herbs. That same aroma, distilled to its essential oil, finds its way into modern perfume manufacture. The Roman naturalist and historian Pliny the Elder wrote of a wine made with hyssop, no doubt a beverage with a distinctive flavor. Centuries later, hyssop was used by medieval monks in the preparation of various liqueurs, notably Chartreuse, still made to this day.

DESCRIPTION. Hyssop makes a bushy plant to 1½ to 2 feet high, well clothed in narrow, smooth leaves that grow opposite one another on woody stems. The leaves are dark, glossy green and possessed of a pungent aroma and resinous flavor. Even at very low temperatures, they're evergreen.

Throughout summer and into autumn, branches bear spikes of small blue-violet blossoms, never a dramatic show but always pleasant. With a bit of searching, you may turn up selections that have flowers of white, pink, or lavender.

Because of its fine texture and general unassertiveness, hyssop is a good foil for herbs with more dramatic foliage or flowers. You can even trim it as a low hedge or use it as one of the "ribbons" in a knot garden.

CULTURE. Grow hyssop in full sun, giving it a well-drained and fairly light soil of neutral to slightly alkaline reaction. Plants tolerate a bit of drought but will thrive with routine watering if drainage is good.

You can start plants from seed sown in early spring. Once established, hyssop may give you a crop of volunteer seedlings in future years. When plants lose their vigor, you can start new ones from stem cuttings in late spring or early summer; this is the best way to perpetuate plants that have particularly special flower colors.

HARVEST & USES. Hyssop has a history of culinary use, but the pungent flavor is not to everyone's liking. At first, use it sparingly. You can add the tender tip growths as a flavoring in salads and soups; the leaves lend a distinctive tang to fruit pies and salads. The oil contained in the leaves helps in the digestion of fatty meats and fish.

LAVENDER

Lavandula species
Labiatae (Mint family)
Perennials; hardiness varies

What romantic associations lavender has! The Victorian and Edwardian elegance of lavender and old lace, lavender perfumes and sachets, languid summers in the south of France.

Native to the Mediterranean region, the lavenders were known to the ancient civilizations of the area. Then, just as now, they were appreciated for their special fragrance. But in Greek and Roman times, the lavender plant that people knew and used was more likely *Lavandula stoechas* (what we call Spanish lavender), rather than the English lavender (*L. angustifolia*) that we associate with the lavender scent.

The Roman use of lavender to perfume bathing water may account for the name, which is said to derive from the Latin *lavare*, to wash.

But the lavender story goes beyond enchanting scent. The aroma we find so attractive is repugnant to insects. Sprigs of lavender placed in drawers and closets are an effective moth repellent, with the bonus of pleasantly scenting the articles they protect.

Lavender also has antibacterial properties, and a sort of lavender water has been used to treat wounds, sores, and burns. The aroma counteracts fainting, while lavender tea has been used to relieve headaches that are brought on by nerves and fatigue.

The unique lavender aroma, though, is the reason for today's commercial production. You'll find the scent in a range of cosmetic items, from soaps to perfumes and lotions.

DESCRIPTION. Lavenders range from large, spreading plants 4 feet high and wide to dwarfs not even a foot tall. You'll find them all delightfully aromatic, but not all alike.

English lavender (*L. angustifolia*, formerly *L. officinalis, L. spica,* and *L. vera*) is the source of the classic lavender scent. The plant sounds a cool, gray note in the landscape, its narrow 2-inch leaves covering a rounded shrub to about 3 feet high. In late spring or early summer, needle-thin stems rise above the foliage mass, topped by tiered whorls of flowers that cluster together into a short spike. Individual flowers are small and, not surprisingly, lavender.

This familiar species is the hardiest one, to about –10°F/ –23°C, and has spawned a number of distinct variations. 'Twickel Purple' is a slightly shorter plant with purple flowers in dense clusters. Three widely available selections grow to about 1½ feet high: 'Hidcote' produces dark purple blossoms in early summer on a narrow-leafed plant; 'Munstead' blooms earlier, bearing dark lavender blue blossoms over green leaves; 'Jean

Davis' is also a green-foliaged plant, its flowers the palest shade of pink.

French lavender (*L. dentata*) is hardy to about 10°F/–12°C. Foliage is dentate: margins of the narrow leaves are edged in square teeth. Dense, billowy plants to 3 feet high have gray-green leaves in one form, purely green leaves in another; foliage is highly aromatic, with a vinegarlike undertone. Lilac purple flowers appear over a long spring-summer period in tight, elongated spikes on gray stems.

Hybrids between English lavender and spike lavender (see facing page) have been designated *L.* x *intermedia*; the common name lavandin has been applied to them to distinguish them from English lavender. In general, these plants are about as hardy as the English lavender parent and are more tolerant of warm, humid summers. The flowering period is a bit later than that of English lavender: early to mid-summer.

Included in this group is 'Provence', the highly aromatic lavender widely cultivated in France for its scent. Plants reach about 2 feet high and wide, bearing narrow gray-green leaves and spikes of pinkish lavender blossoms. Another French selection, 'Grosso', is a compact plant to 2 feet high, presenting its deep purple flowers in tight clusters atop long stems. Similar to 'Provence' is widely available 'Dutch', which circulated for many years as *L. vera*.

Spike lavender (*L. latifolia*) is hardy to about 0°F/–18°C. Think of this as a large English lavender (3 to 4 feet high) with broader leaves; the long, flowering stems frequently branch into several flower spikes.

Spanish lavender (*L. stoechas*) is easily recognized by its blossoms. Small violet flowers are clustered into dense, pineconelike spikes that are topped by conspicuous "rabbit ears" of purple bracts. The basic species is a stocky 1- to 2-foot plant with nearly needlelike gray-green leaves that have a sweetly resinous aroma closer to that of rosemary than English

lavender. It's hardy to about 0°F/–18°C.

The selections 'Atlas', 'Otto Quast' ('Quasti'), and 'Royal Pennant' are more robust plants that have especially large and showy purple bracts. Flowering time is midspring into summer.

CULTURE. The lavenders require full sun and well-drained soil. In the wild, they grow in the poorest-appearing rocky landscapes. Their downfall is humidity accompanied by heat: they'll succeed in cool maritime climates but not in steamy heat.

Set out plants in early spring and water routinely until they become established. Thereafter, moderate watering will suffice. To keep plants compact, shear them after flowering or cut them back in early spring just as new growth begins.

You can easily start new plants from summer cuttings; some lavenders (*L. stoechas*, in particular) will provide you with volunteer seedlings.

HARVEST & USES. You can experiment with fresh lavender leaves in cooking, but it's an acquired taste. You can even make lavender vinegar, sauces, and dressings from the flower spikes.

By far the most common uses of the herb showcase the lavender scent. Dry the flower spikes and use them in potpourris and sachets; or simply place a few in drawers of linens. If you dry the flower spikes attached to long stems, you can use them in arrangements. Pick the flower spikes when they first show color.

'Hidcote' English lavender

LAVENDER COTTON

Santolina species
Compositae (Daisy family)
Perennials; hardy to
–10°F/–23°C

Although lavender cotton, native to Mediterranean lands, surely was known to the various civilizations in the region, records of its use are curiously sparse. Medicinally, it was taken internally as a stimulant and vermifuge; reputed antiseptic qualities accounted for external applications to relieve insect bites and promote the healing of wounds.

More importance may have been attached to the plant's aroma: cut branches effectively repel moths and other insects.

Lavender cotton came rather late to European herb gardens, where it was planted chiefly for decorative purposes.

DESCRIPTION. Inverting its name to cotton lavender, the way it's sometimes seen, makes much sense in describing the character of this plant's foliage. In color and aspect, the plant has a cottony appearance, while the foliage resembles some lavenders.

Both of the two common species (and the variants of one) are useful plants in the foreground of herb gardens and for making small "ribbon" hedges in formal and knot plantings.

Lavender cotton (*Santolina chamaecyparissus*) forms a low, spreading, frothy mound of gray-white foliage. Each very narrow, inch-long leaf is finely divided into feathery segments.

Left to its own devices, a plant will spread outward, its stems arching upward to 12 inches or more; stems root as they spread, so a clump will continue to extend its coverage unless checked occasionally. Perennials nurseries and herb specialists may offer selections, such as 'Nana' and 'Compacta', that are small growing and more compact.

In late spring to early summer, plants are covered with buttonlike, half-inch petalless daisies of a brassy yellow shade.

Similar in many respects is *S. pinnata* and its subspecies, *S. p. neapolitana*. Leaves are a bit longer, their segments more feathery, and the color more gray than white. Flowers are bright yellow; *S. p.* 'Edward Bowles' offers flowers of a pleasing primrose shade.

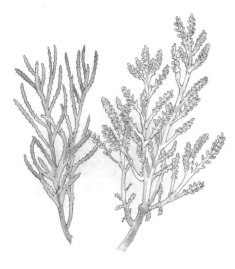

Green lavender cotton (*S. virens*) is similar to standard lavender cotton except for foliage and flower color. Bright green leaves are very narrow, with threadlike segments. The blossoms are a creamy chartreuse.

CULTURE. Even though the lavender cottons hail from warm, dry southern Europe and North Africa, they adapt well to other climates. Chiefly, they need well-drained soil and full sun. They'll tolerate considerable drought but will also take routine watering if drainage is fast.

Shear or cut back plants after flowering to maintain compactness; cut back unkempt plants in spring. Cuttings root easily in spring and summer, but rooted stems usually will supply the need for new plants.

HARVEST & USES. Designers of formal herb gardens value the lavender cottons for hedges and edgings; they take kindly to clipping and shearing, always remaining dense. For household use, you can take advantage of their pungent aroma and use fresh or dried stems in closets and drawers to repel insects.

LEMON BALM

Melissa officinalis
Labiatae (Mint family)
Perennial; hardy to –20°F/–29°C

Unprepossessing lemon balm has, in centuries past, enjoyed quite a reputation for healing and revivifying. Both Pliny and Dioscorides maintained that wounds would heal without infection if lemon balm were applied. And much later, Gerard suggested that the "juice of Balm" would greatly aid the closure of fresh wounds. Modern investigation into various organic essential oils tends to validate, at least in part, these curative applications.

Beverages containing lemon balm were promoted for general revitalization and as a calming agent in cases of distressed nervous systems. The 1696 *London Dispensary* prescribed the inevitable wine-base elixir — in this case, "essence of Balm given in Canary wine" — to be drunk every morning to "renew youth, strengthen the brain, relieve languishing nature, and prevent baldness."

The botanical name *Melissa* comes from the Greek word for bee, and the plant was once well known to beekeepers. Bees will flock to the flowers (making flavorful honey), and it's thought that rubbing the hive with lemon balm leaves will ensure the bees' return.

DESCRIPTION. At first glance, lemon balm closely resembles mint. You see the same square stems with opposing pairs of pointed oval leaves; and, like many mints, the leaf texture is almost quilted.

Clumps of branched stems grow to 2 feet high, bearing loose terminal clusters of small white to creamy yellow flowers during summer. Like its mint relatives, lemon balm will spread vigorously by underground and surface stems.

In the basic species, leaves are a light, bright green with a downy surface. For color contrast in the herb garden, many growers prefer to plant one of the colored-foliage variations. 'Variegata' features green leaves strongly and irregularly variegated in yellow. 'Aurea' and 'All Gold' offer completely golden foliage; the latter has pale lavender flowers.

CULTURE. Lemon balm grows best in good soil that can be kept moist. In mild-summer regions, plants will grow in sun or light shade; where summer is hot, a lightly shaded location is likely to give better results, particularly if you've planted one of the colored-foliage variants.

You can raise lemon balm from seed; established plants will supply volunteer seedlings. Or start new plants from cuttings in late spring and summer or from root divisions during the growing season.

Cut back or shear leggy plants to promote compactness and ensure a supply of young leaves, the ones with the best flavor and aroma.

HARVEST & USES. For drying, pick leaves that are nearly mature or that have just reached full size. The lemonlike scent and flavor deteriorate in older leaves. Dried leaves are an aromatic potpourri ingredient.

You can make a refreshing tea from dried or fresh leaves. The fresh leaves add a pleasant tang to iced drinks, salads, chicken, and mild-flavored fish. In homemade jellies and herb vinegars, they lend an interesting citric undertone.

LEMON VERBENA

Aloysia triphylla
Verbenaceae (Verbena family)
Shrub; hardy to 15°F/–9°C

A native of Argentina and Chile, wonderfully citric lemon verbena languished in the New World for some 300 years after the voyages of discovery before finding its way to the Spanish court in Europe.

As was the case with other lemon-scented herbs, lemon verbena was originally valued for the aroma of its essential oil. And, of course, lemony tea was made from its fresh leaves. When finger bowls were more in vogue than nowadays, some hostesses would add lemon verbena leaves to the water.

DESCRIPTION. With assiduous pinching and pruning, lemon verbena will become a reasonably compact, rounded shrub to 2 to 3 feet high and nearly as wide. But

left to its own devices, the plant is leggy and rangy, bare at the base and growing to 6 or more feet in height.

As a featured specimen, an individual plant will fall short of true beauty. But planted among lower-growing herbs that can mask its gaunt structure, lemon verbena gains in attractiveness. Narrowly lance-shaped, chartreusy green leaves reach 3 to 4 inches long, appearing in whorls of three or four along the stems. The strongly lemony aroma of the leaves is positively mouth watering.

Summer is the flowering season. Individual pinkish white blossoms are quite small, but they're carried in airy clusters that make a pleasing, though subtle, display.

CULTURE. This herb requires a sunny garden with well-drained, reasonably good soil. You can start plants from seed, but germination is slow. Instead, purchase a small plant and set it out in spring after all danger of frost has passed. Or start plants from cuttings taken in late spring or early summer.

Pinch new growth or lightly cut back young stems during the growing season to encourage compactness. In late winter or early spring, about the time new growth begins, you can cut back the plant considerably to encourage more branching in its lower reaches. (If branches have been partially killed by low winter

temperatures, you'll have to prune back to live wood.)

Where winter temperatures drop below 20°F/–7°C, give plants a bit of winter protection; evergreen boughs placed over the base and lower branches will usually keep the plant alive even if freezing temperatures kill a part of the branches. Wherever winter is too cold for lemon verbena's survival in the garden, grow it in a large container that you can move indoors in winter.

HARVEST & USES. To dry leaves and sprigs for maximum scent, harvest them in late spring and early summer, when foliage is near maturity but not old. Use the delightfully aromatic leaves in potpourri and in drawers of linens for a light, lemon-fresh aroma.

You also can brew fresh leaves into a tasty tea or use them as a garnish in iced drinks. A sprig of fresh leaves placed in the bottom of a jar of homemade apple jelly adds a sprightly hint of lemon.

LOVAGE

Levisticum officinale
Umbelliferae (Carrot family)
Perennial; hardy to 0°F/−18°C

Although the name lovage might suggest a connection with amorous pursuits, this herb's history is considerably more prosaic. Native to southern Europe, particularly the Mediterranean countries (*Levisticum* may derive from the Greek name for present-day Liguria), the plant was spread through Europe as the Roman Empire expanded.

Lovage leaves are one of the oldest salad greens. The stems have long been eaten as a vegetable, while both stems and seeds have been candied and consumed as confections.

Herbalists of the 16th century recommended lovage particularly for easing digestive disorders. Lovage tea was one of the medicinal vehicles, though the herb may have been consumed as much for its taste and aroma as for its supposed curative powers. The plant even lent its name to a cordial served in public houses, though the drink also contained tansy and yarrow as flavoring ingredients.

DESCRIPTION. Like angelica, another herb of the carrot family, lovage resembles an overgrown celery plant. Each leaf consists of a long leafstalk from which spring lateral leafstalks bearing jagged-edged leaflets. The glossy, dark green leaves form mounded foliage clumps from which rise hollow stems topped by sprays of flat-topped greenish yellow flower clusters in summer.

Under optimum conditions, a flowering plant may reach 6 feet tall, but the usual height is about half that. The leaves, stalks, and seeds all have a celerylike flavor.

CULTURE. For best growth, choose a sunny site with good soil that can be kept regularly moist. Dig in plenty of organic matter before planting. Full sun is best in most regions, though where summer is very hot, the plants will appreciate light shade in the afternoon.

Sow seeds in the garden in autumn and then thin the plants in spring; or sow seeds in containers and transplant seedlings to the garden in spring. Plants are taprooted, so set them out while they're still fairly small.

Once you have lovage established in your garden, you're likely to get volunteer seedlings that will keep you supplied with new plants. You also can divide established clumps in early spring, replanting segments that show new growth.

HARVEST & USES. All parts of lovage are edible, including the roots. For a supply of leaves year-round, you can dry or freeze the leaves. To save seeds, cut flowering stalks when seeds are ripe and dry them.

Fresh or dried leaves are a tasty ingredient in salads, soups, and white and cheese sauces.

Stems and leafstalks can be prepared in all the ways you would celery; like angelica, the stems can be candied.

Lovage seeds have the same culinary uses as celery seeds. Roots, which can be dug from second- or third-year clumps, can be grated and cooked or added raw to salads.

MARJORAM
(Sweet marjoram)

Origanum majorana
Labiatae (Mint family)
Perennial; hardy to 5°F/–15°C

Sweet marjoram and wild marjoram (*Origanum vulgaris*) have an ancient and intertwined history, both being native — along with other *Origanum* species — to the Mediterranean region. For their historical profiles, see page 75.

DESCRIPTION. Sweet marjoram bears a strong resemblance to its next of kin, oregano, but it's a finer-textured plant with its own distinctive aroma. Plants make tight clumps of upright, branching stems that may be tinted red when young and become semiwoody as they age.

Small oval leaves (less than an inch long) are light green with grayish green undersides; usually, they're boat or scoop shaped (edges higher than midrib) rather than flat. Small white flowers grow from knotlike, four-sided clusters of tiny leaves at stem tips.

CULTURE. As would be expected of a plant that comes from the sunny Mediterranean, sweet marjoram requires full sun. Give it well-drained soil of average quality and water routinely.

You can raise sweet marjoram from seeds planted in early spring; or start new plants from divisions at that time or from cuttings in late spring or summer.

Where climate lets sweet marjoram live from year to year, the plants will become semi-shrubby and congested. To keep them compact, cut them back or shear them in early spring. Cut out the twiggy growth and cut back the remaining strong stems at least halfway.

Where sweet marjoram won't survive outside during winter, treat it as an annual (starting new plants each year) or grow it in a container and move it indoors in winter.

HARVEST & USES. The leaves, fresh or dried, have a sweetly pungent aroma and flavor. To use fresh leaves, pick them as needed. For drying, pick leaves just before plants flower. You also can freeze leaves.

Sweet marjoram is a favorite culinary herb found in Mediterranean and Middle Eastern cuisines. Use the fresh or dried leaves in meat dishes and salads. Make a tea from fresh leaves, use them to make herb vinegar, or try them as a flavoring in fruit jelly. Dried leaves are a common potpourri ingredient.

Sweet Marjoram Scones

1½ cups all-purpose flour
½ cup whole wheat flour
½ teaspoon each salt and baking soda
1 tablespoon chopped fresh marjoram or 1 teaspoon dry marjoram
2 teaspoons baking powder
2 tablespoons sugar
¼ cup butter or margarine, cut into chunks
½ cup currants
¾ cup buttermilk

In a food processor or bowl, whirl or stir all-purpose flour, whole wheat flour, salt, baking soda, marjoram, baking powder, and sugar until combined. Add butter; whirl or rub with your fingers until coarse crumbs form. Add currants; whirl or stir just until evenly distributed. Add buttermilk and whirl or stir just until evenly moistened.

Turn dough out onto a board lightly coated with all-purpose flour and knead 12 turns. On a greased 12- by 15-inch baking sheet, pat dough into a 6½-inch round. With a knife, score dough into 8 wedges. Bake in a 425° oven until well browned (25 to 30 minutes). Makes 4 to 8 servings.

MINT

Mentha species
Labiatae (Mint family)
Perennials; most hardy to about
−20°F/−29°C

According to ancient Greek legend, the nubile nymph Menthe turned the head of Pluto, lord of the underworld. Inconveniently, Pluto was married and his wife, Persephone, took a dim view of this attraction — so dim, in fact, that she used her own other-worldly powers to turn the unwitting youth into a lowly plant that forevermore would be inconspicuous and underfoot. So much for competition!

Small consolation, perhaps, but Menthe's loss was our gain: the various minty fragrances and flavors have been favorites of mortals ever since the unlucky girl sprouted leaves. The Greeks and Romans used mint to flavor wines and even made a kind of mint sauce. The scent was a good mouth freshener. The Greeks, and later the Muslims, believed mint encouraged amorousness and virility.

Understandably, mint was a favored strewing herb, its volatile oils masking less pleasant odors while also repelling unwelcome pests. Reputed medicinal qualities (some now scientifically proven) led to its use as an antiseptic, an aid to digestion, and a soothing agent for bronchial troubles.

Conquering Romans took Mediterranean spearmint to the British Isles, and centuries later the Pilgrims brought mints to the New World, where they willingly naturalized. Today, the mint flavor and scent are found in diverse items, from chewing gum and toothpaste to cough drops and liqueurs.

DESCRIPTION. Mint species are numerous and they've added to their number by producing notable hybrid offspring. All have stems that are square in cross section (typical of the mint family) and produce small flowers that are borne in whorls toward stem tips.

Golden apple mint (*Mentha gentilis*) displays yellow variegations that radiate from the centers of smooth green leaves that are tinged with an apple aroma. Another name for this plant, ginger mint, describes the flavor overtone. Plants reach about 2 feet high; flowers are inconspicuous.

Peppermint (*M. piperita*) is a robust 3-foot-high plant with 3-inch leaves featuring the familiar scent and flavor; flowers are purple. Plants spread rapidly and can become invasive. Orange mint (*M. p.* 'Citrata'), also called bergamot or eau-de-cologne mint, combines the characteristic aroma and flavor with a dash of orange. Plants reach about 2 feet high, bearing broad, 2-inch dark green, purple-edged leaves on red-purple stems. Flowers are lavender.

M. p. 'Crispa' presents a strong peppermint scent from crinkled, laciniated green leaves carried on purple stems.

Pennyroyal (*M. pulegium*) is hardy to about 0°F/−18°C. Its

Pineapple mint

MINT . . .

ground-hugging plants are covered in oval, ½-inch bright green leaves with strong scent and flavor. Used sparingly, they can flavor foods and beverages; in quantity, they're toxic. Given shade and moisture, pennyroyal grows well between paving stones.

Jewel mint of Corsica (M. *requienii*) is hardy to about 5°F/–15°C. The smallest of the mints, this creeping plant reaches no more than ½ inch high and features tiny rounded leaves that look like moss. Appropriately tiny light purple flowers decorate the carpet in summer.

Plant this mint in a container or between paving stones, where footfalls will release its pungent, pepperminty scent. Give it plenty of moisture in sun or light shade (shade is necessary where summer is hot). In cold winters, the foliage disappears.

Spearmint (M. *spicata)* is the source of the familiar chewing-gum flavor and is the favorite for making mint jelly. Plants are upright, to 1½ to 2 feet high, and, compared with peppermint, have slightly smaller, lance-shaped to oval leaves with a quilted appearance. Whorls of lavender flowers are spaced so closely as to give the impression of a flower spike.

Like peppermint, this is an aggressive grower. Herb nurseries may carry variants on the species, including one with distinctly narrower foliage and purplish stems. The selection 'Crispa'

('Crispata') has leaves that are elaborately fringed and laced.

Apple mint (M. *suaveolens,* formerly M. *rotundifolia*) is an upright plant to perhaps 2½ feet high, its stems and rounded grayish green leaves covered in downy hairs. Whorls of lilac-white flowers are closely spaced to form short spikes. A subtle apple scent combines with the mint aroma.

In contrast, pineapple mint (M. *s.* 'Variegata') brings a tropical-fruit fragrance to the white-marbled leaves; plants are a bit smaller than those of apple mint.

CULTURE. Give mints a sunny to lightly shaded location, but avoid full sun where summer tends to be hot.

In general, the mints are easy to grow, given regular moisture and a not-too-heavy, organically enriched soil. Some would say they're too easy to grow, several being notoriously invasive even under imperfect conditions. To curb such rambunctiousness, grow mints in containers or confine them with a surround of wood or masonry. You can pinch or cut back stems to counteract leggy growth.

All of the larger mints are easy to propagate from stem cuttings or by layering, but this is seldom necessary because rooted runners can be detached and planted separately. With the two ground cover types, it's easier to take small patches to start a new planting.

When the clump becomes sparse and unattractive, divide and replant any mint in spring.

HARVEST & USES. Pick mint leaves as needed during the growing season to use fresh. To dry, you can place individual leaves on trays; or cut stems and hang them in bunches upside down. You can even pick fresh leaves, place them in plastic bags, and freeze them for later use.

Savor the various mints in tea and jelly (to make mint jelly, see page 106), as a garnish in beverages, and as a piquant accent in salads and desserts (the flavor combines well with ice cream, chocolate, and cheesecake). Leaves can be sugared and used as edible decoration. Mint sprigs contribute distinctive flavor to herb vinegar. Mint is especially popular in recipes from Greece and the Middle East.

Tabbouli

1 cup each bulgur wheat and cold water
½ cup each minced parsley and green onions
¼ cup chopped green bell pepper
¼ cup chopped fresh mint or 2 tablespoons dry mint
1 large tomato, finely diced
¼ cup each olive oil and lemon juice
Salt
Tomato wedges

Combine bulgur and cold water in a bowl; let stand for 1 hour. Drain any liquid that is not absorbed.

In a large bowl, mix bulgur, parsley, onions, bell pepper, mint, diced tomato, oil, and lemon juice. Season to taste with salt. Cover and refrigerate for at least 1 hour or up to 3 days.

Mound tabbouli in a serving bowl and arrange tomatoes on top. Makes 6 to 8 servings.

MULLEIN

Verbascum species
Scrophulariaceae (Figwort
family)
Biennials, perennials; hardy to
−20°F/−29°C

In ancient times, mullein was
much more than a stately wildflower. From the Mediterranean
to the Far East, it was thought
the plant would ward off evil
spirits and thwart magic spells.
Thus, it was mullein that Homer
carried with him to protect him-
self against Circe's sorcery.

Of the various mulleins,
great mullein (*Verbascum thapsus*) was the most widely used.
Medicinally, it appeared in
preparations to ease coughing
and congestion.

Its most conspicuous use,
however, was as a primitive can-
dle. The dried stems, dipped in
suet or tallow, could be ignited to
make impressive torches.

DESCRIPTION. Like foxgloves, their relatives, the
mulleins are showy, stately plants
with tall flower spires rising from
low clumps of large, coarse
leaves. But the resemblance ends
there. Unlike the foxgloves'
familiar thimblelike flowers,
mullein blossoms are flat and circular, reminiscent of single roses.

Great mullein is a biennial,
forming in its first year a rosette
of soft, foot-long gray-green
leaves. In late spring and summer
of the plant's second year, it
sends up a straight, leafy stem to
about 6 feet, the upper third to
half of which becomes a dense
spike of inch-wide yellow flowers.

The spherical seed capsules
that follow flowering will provide
an ample supply of volunteer
seedlings for another floral show
2 years hence.

Seed catalogs and perennials
specialists offer other *Verbascum*
species and hybrids that resemble
V. thapsus. Among the perennials
you'll find a range of flower colors, including pink, purple,
white, and reddish shades along
with the prevalent yellow.

CULTURE. All mulleins are
tough and undemanding plants:
give them a well-drained, not-
too-rich soil and grow them on
the dry side.

Biennial species die after
flowering and setting seed; save
the seeds to continue raising
plants. If you fail to harvest stalks
before seeds scatter, you'll get
volunteer seedlings that are a
nuisance to weed out because of
their deep taproots.

When you grow different
mulleins near one another, you
may get hybrid offspring that
won't exactly resemble either
parent. Likewise, seedlings of
hybrids are likely not to repro-
duce the parent in appearance.
To increase favorite individuals
of perennials, take root cuttings
or carefully separate young rooted rosettes from the clump.

HARVEST & USES. The
mulleins appear in gardens strictly as decorative plants.

NASTURTIUM

Tropaeolum species
Tropaeoloaceae (Nasturtium family)
Perennials grown as annuals

Unlike the majority of herbs, whose pedigrees can be traced to ancient civilizations, nasturtium has no known history. Surely, its conspicuous flowers in yellow and orange might have evoked a sun god or its earthly incarnation. But whatever colorful history these plants may have had in their South American homeland is buried with the Incas who once populated that area.

Nasturtiums were introduced to European horticulture in the late 1600s; their edible-herbal uses didn't come to light until later. And, to confuse matters a bit, the plant known botanically as *Nasturtium* is watercress, the main ingredient in tea sandwiches. For this reason, some Europeans refer to our brightly flowered nasturtium flowers as Indian cress.

DESCRIPTION. The colorful nasturtiums — vinelike *Tropaeolum majus*, bushy *T. minus*, and, more importantly, the modern selections and hybrids — are usually grown for the flashy flowers they produce over a long season.

Although sizes and growth habits differ, all annual nasturtiums fit one general description. A leaf is virtually round and shieldlike, held at the end of a long leafstalk that attaches off-center to the leaf. The 2-inch flower is shaped like a horn, with a long spur at one end opening out into a bell shape at the other. Flower colors range from creamy white to maroon, including yellow, orange, red, red-brown, and pink.

Two species are the ancestors of today's nasturtiums. Climbing (or trailing) *T. majus* extends lax stems to about 6 feet, climbing upward by coiling its leafstalks around any slender support. Plants of *T. minus*, in contrast, remain bushy to about 15 inches high and wide.

Among the hybrid strains available are both trailing and bushy plants, some with semi-double to double blossoms.

CULTURE. Few plants are easier to grow than nasturtiums, which makes them particular favorites with novice gardeners of all ages. The large seeds make for easy planting, as shown on page 30; sow them where you want the plants, since seedlings don't transplant well.

The best growing conditions for nasturtiums are a sunny bed with rather light soil (overly fertile soil produces leaves at the expense of flowers) and a regular supply of water.

Nasturtiums are at their best in climates that are cool to moderate in summer; hot weather, especially when accompanied by high humidity, does them in. In low-desert regions, you can plant seeds in autumn for good performance all winter and until weather starts to heat up in spring.

In cool and virtually frost-free regions, plants will be perennial; and anywhere they're grown, they'll likely maintain their presence by volunteer seedlings.

HARVEST & USES. Both leaves and flowers have a pleasant, peppery flavor not unlike watercress. Use them to perk up and add beautiful color to any mixed green salad. Pick the pea-size seeds before they ripen and pickle them to produce an acceptable substitute for capers.

OREGANO
(Wild marjoram)

Origanum vulgare
Labiatae (Mint family)
Perennial; hardy to –20°F/–29°C

All the *Origanum* species were well known to ancient civilizations, where they probably served as culinary herbs. Common oregano, sometimes called wild marjoram, was valued in ancient times as an antidote to certain poisons and to convulsions.

Legend has it that sweet marjoram (see page 70) was created by Aphrodite, goddess of love and beauty. Wreaths of marjoram stems were worn by bridal couples to ensure happiness, and the presence of the plant growing on a grave signified contentment of the departed's soul.

During the Middle Ages, the marjorams were valued for their scent. Leaves carried in nosegays or "sweet bags" (a sort of primitive sachet) would give instant relief from disagreeable odors.

DESCRIPTION. Oregano resembles sweet marjoram, but the distinguishing features are easy to spot. Oregano leaves are broadly ovate to almost heart shaped and are larger and flatter than those of sweet marjoram. Stems rise from a clump of leaves to 2 to 2½ feet tall, branching a bit toward their tips.

Small flowers are usually purplish pink, each with five equal segments, and come in clusters at the ends of stems and branches. Unlike sweet marjoram, which makes a compact clump, oregano spreads by underground stems to form small colonies.

From herb specialists you may be able to obtain several variant selections, such as 'Compactum' (to about 15 inches tall), the even lower 'Compactum Nanum', and yellow-leafed 'Aureum'. Forms with white flowers may also be available. One is called winter oregano, properly *O. vulgare hirtum*, though you may find it labeled *O. heracleoticum*.

Pot marjoram (*O. onites*) grows to a bushy 1½ feet high, with bright green leaves, red stems, and lavender to white flowers. Its flavor is less appealing than either sweet marjoram or oregano; herb specialists often carry its attractive golden-leafed variant, *O. onites* 'Aureum'.

Herb growers sometimes list other kinds of "oregano" —

totally unrelated plants but containing the same essential oils present in the *Origanum* species. Among these are two Mexican oreganos: *Lippia graveolens*, a frost-tender shrub, and *Poliomintha longiflora*, a 2- to 3-foot shrub hardy to about 20°F/–7°C.

CULTURE. Except for forms with yellow or variegated leaves, oregano revels in full sun. Give it well-drained, good soil (slightly alkaline is preferred) and water plants moderately. You can start plants from seed, from cuttings taken in late spring or summer, or from divisions in early spring. Cut out spent flowering stems in autumn.

About every 3 years you should divide crowded clumps in early spring and replant healthy, rooted segments.

HARVEST & USES. Oregano appears in many different cuisines and in a variety of dishes. Use fresh leaves throughout the growing season. Dry or freeze leaves to use when fresh leaves aren't available.

ORIENTAL HERBS

The peoples of the Far East — especially those in China, India, and Southeast Asia — employ a diverse assortment of herbs both in medicine and in cooking. Although some of the foods used in Asian dishes are exotic to Western tastes, it's usually the herbs that impart the distinctive flavor.

On these two pages are five culinary herbs often found in Asian cooking. Each can bring a unique taste and aroma to your own cooking.

CUMIN

Cuminum cyminum
Umbelliferae (Carrot family)
Annual

Although of Mediterranean origin, cumin has established itself quite firmly in Asian cuisines. The seeds (the only part of the plant that's used) are one component in curry preparations; they're also used in chutneys, various meat dishes, and some baked goods. (Aficionados of Mexican food will recognize cumin, too.)

In common with its many carrot family relatives, the cumin plant bears tiny white flowers in flattened clusters. In size, it's on a par with parsley, but the finely dissected leaves recall fennel.

Plants need a long, hot growing season to mature their seeds. Sow seeds, after all danger of frost is past, directly in the garden. Choose a sunny location where soil is well drained and fairly light. Thin plants to about 12 inches apart. Water routinely until seeds ripen; then harvest and dry. Store seeds in an airtight container and use them whole or crushed.

FENUGREEK

Trigonella foenum-graecum
Leguminosae (Pea family)
Annual

Like cumin, fenugreek originated in the Mediterranean region, where it lends its distinctive flavor to the Middle Eastern candy *halvah*. This is a useful plant, not only as a flavoring for food but also as a cosmetic, a medicine, and a fodder for livestock. In cooking, the seeds flavor curry powder, and the leaves contribute a flavor similar to fresh green beans to salads.

Fenugreek's trifoliate leaves, appearing on upright, slightly branched plants that can reach 2 feet high, suggest clover. Flowers

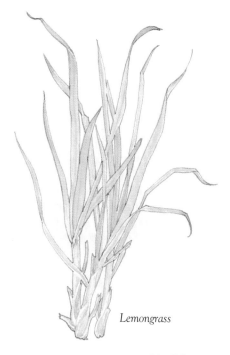

Lemongrass

are inconsequential; they're creamy white and sweet pea shaped. Long, narrow beanlike capsules contain the edible seeds.

Sow fenugreek seeds directly in the garden, choosing well-drained soil and a sunny location. Water plants routinely. Seed capsules can be harvested 3 to 4 months after flowering. Dry them in paper bags; later, separate the seeds from the capsules.

GINGER

Zingiber officinale
Zingiberaceae (Ginger family)
Perennial; hardy to 28°F/–2°C

It's the rhizomes of this plant, the plain cousin to the flashy kahili ginger of Hawaii, that provide the well-known ginger flavor. Elongated and thick, they send up canelike stems 2 to 4 feet high, bearing foot-long, lance-shaped leaves of glossy bright green. Greenish yellow flowers appear at stem tips only where the growing season is long, hot, and moist.

Cumin

As a native of the Tropics, ginger needs a long growing season, plenty of water, light shade from hot sun, and a virtually frostless winter. In climates too cold for its outdoor survival year-round, grow ginger in the garden and treat it as an annual crop, harvesting all by autumn; or store rhizomes over the winter as you would dahlias or cannas.

An alternative is to grow ginger in large containers of organically enriched soil and move them to a frost-free spot during the coldest months.

To start ginger, simply plant the fresh roots you buy at the grocery store: cut them into 2-inch sections (making sure each piece has visible growth buds) and place them just beneath the soil's surface. Water heavily once growth begins.

After several months, when rhizomes have gained in size, you can begin harvesting as you need roots for cooking. Peel and slice or grate the fresh roots and use them in curries and other Asian dishes.

LEMONGRASS

Cymbopogon citratus
Gramineae (Grass family)
Perennial; hardy to 28°F/–2°C

The name lemongrass perfectly describes the plant: it's a grass with a lemony aroma and flavor.

Given long, hot summers and plenty of water — the conditions it enjoys in its native Southeast Asia — lemongrass will develop into graceful, fountainlike clumps to 3 feet high composed of ½-inch-wide leaves.

Lemongrass Marinade

2   tablespoons chopped fresh or dry lemongrass
1   onion, quartered
3   cloves garlic
3   tablespoons sugar
2   tablespoons roasted peanuts
1   tablespoon fish sauce or soy sauce
1½ teaspoons pepper
1   teaspoon Chinese five-spice; or ¼ teaspoon each ground cloves, crushed anise seeds, ground cinnamon, ground allspice, and ground ginger

If using dry lemongrass, soak in hot water for 30 minutes. Drain well. Combine lemongrass, onion, garlic, sugar, peanuts, fish sauce, pepper, and five-spice in a food processor or blender. Whirl until smooth. Makes enough for 2 pounds meat.

In nontropical gardens, expect a 1- to 2-foot height, the clumps growing to about a foot across.

Lemongrass is typically used to flavor soups, fish dishes, and tea, or as a marinade for meat; all it takes is a few inches of the fresh or dried herb. The bulbous base of each plant, which looks like a large green onion, possesses an even stronger lemon flavor than the leaves, with mild onion-garlic overtones.

Peel the tough outer layer from lemongrass and trim. Crush, chop, or thinly slice the stalks.

SHISO

Perilla frutescens
Labiatae (Mint family)
Annual

In appearance, shiso resembles a large basil (or a coleus, another relative), but its flavor suggests a combination of mint and cinnamon. You can use the leaves as a seasoning or as a salad component; in Japan, you'll find shiso used in tempura, in bean curd preparations, and in fish dishes.

Robust and fast growing, the plant is an attractive garden ornament. It makes a bushy foliage mass to 2 to 3 feet high, bearing broadly oval, textured leaves. Some forms have green leaves, others have bronzy purple leaves, and one strain (Fancy Fringes) has purple leaves with elaborately curled and cut margins. Insignificant white flowers come in branched spikes.

Give shiso sun or light shade, well-drained average soil, and routine watering. Sow seeds either in containers for transplanting or directly where you want the plants. If you let plants go to seed, you'll have volunteer seedlings for next year's crop.

Fancy Fringes shiso

ORRIS ROOT

Iris pallida, I. x *germanica*
'Florentina'
Iridaceae (Iris family)
Perennials; hardy to
–30°F/–34°C

It should come as no surprise that a plant as beautiful as the iris would have a fragrant rootstock that, when dried and ground to a powder called "orris root," lends its scent to perfume.

Iris, the goddess of the rainbow, gave her name to this showy-flowered and colorfully varied group of plants. Many different irises grow in the Mediterranean region, where the conspicuous flowers were esteemed by the area's ancient inhabitants. Wall paintings from Egyptian times document the presence of irises in gardens beginning in the reign of Thutmose III.

Iris x *germanica* 'Florentina'

But it wasn't until Greek and Roman times that the plant was used as an important ingredient in perfumery. Production involves digging mature rhizomes, skinning them, and drying them for up to 3 years, during which time a violetlike aroma develops. The thoroughly dry rhizomes are then ground to a powder used also as a fixative in potpourri.

DESCRIPTION. The traditional sources of orris root are two irises found in Italy, the adjacent Dalmatian coast, and southward into northern Greece.

The first, *Iris pallida,* varies in size throughout its native range, but the flowers are typically lavender to light violet, carried on closely branched stems to 2 to 3½ feet tall. Swordlike leaves are bluish green with a noticeable "bloom" on the surface.

Specialty iris growers sometimes offer selected forms, principally 'Pallida Variegata' (almost always incorrectly cataloged as 'Zebra' or *I. pallida* 'Variegata'), which has foliage conspicuously striped in yellow to creamy white; flowers are a darker violet blue on stems that rise to about 2 feet high.

The second, *I.* x *germanica* 'Florentina', flowers slightly earlier than *I. pallida,* its blue-tinted, elongated flowers coming on shorter and more widely branched stems. Compared with *I. pallida,* the rhizomes of 'Florentina' are more elongated, and the foliage is slightly greener.

CULTURE. Give irises a sunny position in any sort of soil, from sandy to claylike, as long as it's well drained. Rhizomes will rot if soil around them remains saturated for long.

Set out rhizomes in early summer to early autumn, opting for the earlier time in colder-winter regions. Water routinely during the period from first growth in spring to about 6 weeks after flowering; thereafter, moderate water is enough.

Divide clumps (at the best planting time for your area) when they become crowded and performance declines, usually after 3 or 4 years.

HARVEST & USES. Although you can try producing your own orris root, it's far simpler to purchase it. Grow irises for their unrivaled beauty and color.

PARSLEY

Petroselenium crispum
Umbelliferae (Carrot family)
Biennial grown as an annual

The ancient Greeks would be astonished to see us eating parsley. In their time, the herb was associated with death and was used as a ceremonial decoration, not as a food. Such customs, however, weren't passed on to the Romans, who not only included it in a variety of dishes but also consumed it to counteract the effects of wine and of garlic on the breath.

Centuries later, herbalists recommended parsley as a digestive aid and diuretic; applied to the skin, it was credited with alleviating bruises.

DESCRIPTION. Nearly everyone is familiar with parsley, the green garnish that usually gets pushed to the side of the plate.

Like other herbs in the carrot family, an individual parsley leaf consists of a leafstalk, its side branches, and numerous separate leaflets. The leaflets are tufted and finely cut, with serrated or toothed edges and wrinkled surfaces. A single leafstalk and its leaflets look a little like a bonsai.

Foliage mass grows to 6 to 12 inches high, making parsley attractive in clumps or as an edging. Flower stalks form in the second year, growing to 2 feet high and bearing flattened clusters of tiny greenish flowers. Vegetable-seed specialists offer named selections with especially ornate leaves.

Italian, or plain-leafed, parsley (*Petroselenium crispum neapolitanum*) is a larger plant with a less complicated leaf but a more intense flavor. Individual leaves are like a small version of celery. Hamburg parsley (*P. c. tuberosum*) produces an edible carrot-like root that can be cooked as a vegetable or used raw in salads.

CULTURE. Parsley will take the best soil you can give it and requires full sun, except in hot-summer regions where it likes a bit of shade in the afternoon. Sow seeds directly in the ground during April in cold-winter regions, from December through May where winter is mild; in the low desert, sow in early autumn.

To enhance germination, soak seeds in warm water for 24 hours before planting. Later, thin seedlings to 6 to 8 inches apart. Most growers start a new crop each year, as second-year leaves are unpalatable.

HARVEST & USES. Generally, parsley leaves are used fresh, picked as you need them. But you can dry or freeze the leaves for later use. Harvest leaves before plants flower: once flower stalks form, the leaves' flavor becomes bitter.

As a garnish, chopped parsley turns up regularly in salads, soups, egg dishes, and vegetables. In cooking, it's used in a wide variety of foods.

Pasta with Parsley-Lemon Pesto

1 pound penne or other dry pasta shape
1 large lemon
2 cups lightly packed chopped fresh parsley
2 cloves garlic
3 ounces (about ¾ cup) grated Parmesan cheese
3 tablespoons olive oil
Coarsely ground pepper

Cook pasta in boiling water until al dente. Meanwhile, use a vegetable peeler to pare zest from lemon in large strips. In a food processor, whirl lemon zest, parsley, garlic, and Parmesan until finely minced.

Drain pasta and place in a warm bowl. Add parsley mixture and oil; toss well. Season to taste with pepper. Makes 4 to 6 servings.

POT MARIGOLD
(Calendula)

Calendula officinalis
Compositae (Daisy family)
Annual

Countless gardeners are very familiar with pot marigold; yet few know that until recent times, it was regarded as a healing and culinary herb and was also used as decoration and as a source of yellow dye.

The surviving folk name, pot marigold, attests to the plant's former culinary importance, pot being short for pottage, a kind of vegetable stew. Both flowers and leaves appeared in edible preparations, the petals adding color to such pale fare as custard, butter, certain cheeses, and rice.

Medicinal applications were varied, according to old herbals. The yellow to orange flower color led believers in the Doctrine of Signatures to consider the plant effective in treating jaundice. Preparations were applied to cuts and skin irritations.

In more recent times, some of these claims have been validated. During the Civil War and even World War I, pot marigold leaves were used to staunch the flow of blood from battle wounds.

DESCRIPTION. The average gardener knows this plant as calendula, a popular choice when you want masses of bright color during the cooler times of year.

In mild-winter regions, its warm-hued flowers blaze from autumn through winter into spring. The name calendula, in fact, is derived from *calends*, the first day of every month in the Roman calendar, in recognition of the plant's long flowering period in mild climates. Where winter is characterized by freezing temperatures and snow, its flowering season is spring to midsummer, when it finally succumbs to heat and humidity.

Plants are bushy, to 1 to 3 feet high, with rather narrow, long leaves that are aromatic and slightly sticky. The double to semidouble daisy flowers (one to a stem) reach 2½ to 4 inches across; plant breeders have expanded the color range to include cream, yellow, gold, orange, and apricot.

Hybrid strains are available; these include dwarf kinds to 12 inches high and those that have flowers with dark centers or quilled petals.

CULTURE. Sun-loving pot marigold will grow in a range of soils, but best performance is achieved in good soil with decent drainage.

Where winters are cold, you can start seeds indoors (they take about a week to germinate) and transplant seedlings to the garden 6 to 8 weeks later for bloom until summer heat finishes them. In milder regions, sow outdoors in July or August for bloom by the December holidays, or in late summer to early autumn for spring bloom.

Nurseries and garden centers usually have a ready supply of young plants. Remove spent blossoms to keep plants productive. If you let flowers produce seeds, you'll get volunteer seedlings the next year.

HARVEST & USES. The edible flower petals have a slightly tangy taste that enhances salads, soups, rice, fish, and egg dishes. Cooked with rice, the petals impart a saffron color, though not the saffron flavor, to the grains. Chopped young leaves can be used in salads.

Pick flowers when they're open but before they age. Dry the flower petals to have them available all year for cooking or potpourri.

PURPLE CONEFLOWER

Echinacea purpurea
Compositae (Daisy family)
Perennial; hardy to –35°F/–37°C

Retrace the history of many of today's familiar herbs and you find yourself among Egyptian pyramids, Biblical sites, or marble temples. Go back with purple coneflower and you encounter endless sweeps of prairie grass, vast herds of bison, and nomadic Indian tribes.

Although Native Americans may have regarded it as a pretty flower, as we do today, they looked upon it first and foremost as a source of potent medicine. European settlers of North America found the indigenous people using purple coneflower to treat a variety of toxic bites, from insect stings to more dangerous snakebites. They chewed the plant's roots to ease the pain of toothaches.

Even more sweeping are the properties in the plant that help the body resist infectious diseases. Contemporary research, spurred by a history of effective folk remedy, has determined that species of *Echinacea* have the ability to increase the body's production of interferon, thereby aiding the immune system in combating a variety of diseases, including the flu. Moreover, the antiseptic properties recognized by modern researchers in purple coneflower bear out its use by Native Americans in treating external infections, such as boils and abscesses.

DESCRIPTION. Anyone familiar with black-eyed Susan (*Rudbeckia*) will recognize purple coneflower as its close cousin. The blossoms are virtually the same — large daisies with beehivelike brownish purple centers — but in this plant the petals are rosy purple. Typically, the petals of these 4-inch flowers bend downward from the center, giving flowers a forlorn look.

Perennials specialists offer various named selections, such as 'Bright Star', in which the petals stand outward in circular outline, as well as those with petals of pink, rosy red, or white, and centers that range from orange to bronze.

The showy flowers appear in midsummer on sparsely leafed stems that reach 2½ to 4 feet high; each stem usually bears just one flower. Stems rise from a clump of 4- to 8-inch oval leaves with a sandpapery surface.

CULTURE. Purple coneflower gives you a colorful display, yet demands little in return. A sunny location is always suitable, though in hot-summer regions the plants will succeed in partial shade. They need a well-drained soil of just average fertility. Although established clumps will tolerate some drought, you'll get the best performance if plants receive moderate watering.

When clumps become crowded (usually in about 4 years' time), dig and divide them in early spring or autumn.

HARVEST & USES. Despite its history of medicinal use and the current interest in its properties, purple coneflower is simply a decorative component of the herb garden. The dried seed heads look attractive in dried flower arrangements.

ROSE

Rosa species
Rosaceae (Rose family)
Shrubs; hardy to –30°F/–34°C

Surprised to learn that roses are herbs? The common name for *Rosa gallica officinalis* — Apothecary Rose — is clear indication of a usefulness beyond that of sheer beauty.

From the time of the ancient Greeks, roses have been favored plants, symbolizing beauty, love, fidelity, and happiness. The writings of Confucius from about the same period mention extensive rose plantings. Romans lavished rose petals and blossoms on festive occasions, ate rose-petal confections, and drank rose-petal wine; medications were prepared from petals and hips.

As symbols, roses were taken up by the early Christian church (think of the Rosary) and were a popular heraldic motif. England's War of the Roses involved the royal houses of York and Lancaster, whose emblems were, respectively, a white and a red rose.

Apothecary Rose

Today, certain rose petals are processed to extract rose oil used in perfumery and as a scenting agent in cosmetics.

DESCRIPTION. Hundreds of rose species exist, and tens of thousands of named selections and hybrids have been distributed in the past 200 years. But several roses are significant for their long history.

Apothecary Rose bears semi-double, cherry-crimson blossoms with contrasting yellow stamens. The plant is well foliaged, growing to 3 to 4 feet high. 'Rosa Mundi' (*R. gallica versicolor*) is simply a color variation of Apothecary Rose; flowers show crimson and palest pink, displayed in stripes, dashes, and stipples.

Damask roses include spring-flowering Summer Damask (*R.* x *damascena*), repeat-flowering Autumn Damask (*R.* x *d. semperflorens*), and various named selections that are grown for the production of rose oil. Autumn Damask, also known as Rose of Castile, makes a large, thorny, open plant with light yellowish gray-green leaves; slender buds open to highly scented, loosely formed clear pink flowers.

Eglantine (*R. eglanteria*) is noted particularly for its dark green leaves, which have an apple aroma. Plants are vigorous, rather fountainlike, growing to 12 feet high; single pink blossoms appear in late spring, followed by red-orange fruits.

CULTURE. Roses perform best in good, well-drained soil. They require full sun and routine watering. Set out bare-root plants in late autumn or early spring (cold-winter climates) or during winter (milder-winter regions).

Commercial growers offer roses budded onto other rootstocks or, in some cases, grown on their own roots; the *R. gallica* roses, in particular, form large colonies of suckering stems when grown on their own roots. Prune as needed to shape plants; remove unproductive and dead wood just before growth starts in late winter or early spring.

HARVEST & USES. For centuries, rose petals have been dried and enjoyed for their fragrance, notably in potpourri.

For culinary use, steep them in water to make rose water or a rose syrup, or steep in wine or vinegar to impart a delicate flavor. You can scatter fresh petals as edible garnish on fruit salads (first remove the bitter white heel of each petal). You can also sugar them to decorate confections.

ROSEMARY

Rosmarinus officinalis
Labiatae (Mint family)
Shrub; hardy to 0°F/–18°C

In ancient times, rosemary was a culinary seasoning herb just as it is now. But its associations with fidelity and memory gave it a particular importance. Rosemary was found at weddings and funerals, and it was worn by students cramming for exams. Disinfectant powers were attributed to it, accounting for its presence in jails and sickrooms.

DESCRIPTION. Rounded plants grow to 3 to 4 feet high and a bit spreading but irregular in outline, with main branches that tend to sweep outward and upward. Narrow, almost needle-like 1-inch leaves usually are glossy green on their upper surfaces, grayish white beneath, and distinctly aromatic (somewhat

pinelike) when bruised or brushed.

Small clusters of ¼- to ½-inch flowers appear over a long bloom period that usually begins in winter and extends into spring, but which may start as early as autumn. The typical flower color is lavender blue, but specialty nurseries may offer white-flowered individuals and the lavender rose variant 'Mallorca Pink'.

Other named selections vary in growth habit, plant size, and shade of blue flowers. The best-known low-growing rosemary is 'Prostratus'. Its initial growth is horizontal, but secondary stems may arch upward and then curve or twist back toward the ground. One plant can cover considerable territory, rooting as it spreads and building to 1½ to 2 feet in height. Flowers are light grayish blue. Widely sold 'Tuscan Blue' becomes a strongly upright 6-foot plant.

CULTURE. Rosemary needs well-drained soil and little else. With good drainage, plants will accept regular watering, but they'll thrive with little or no supplemental water in all but the hottest-summer regions.

Set out young plants in autumn, winter, or early spring. In cold-winter regions, grow rosemary in containers and move plants indoors during winter. You can root cuttings from semihardened new growth in spring or early summer. Branches that

touch the ground usually form roots and can be moved to become independent plants.

Prune as needed to shape or direct growth.

HARVEST & USES. Pick fresh leaves as you need them for cooking; or dry cut stems, strip the leaves, and store them in airtight containers. Rosemary complements many meat dishes (particularly lamb), stews, and vegetables. Use sprigs as decoration.

Orange-Rosemary Sorbet

½ cup water
2 tablespoons sugar
1 teaspoon finely chopped fresh rosemary or ¼ teaspoon finely chopped dry rosemary
2 cups orange juice

In a 1- to 2-quart pan, bring water, sugar, and rosemary to a boil over high heat; reduce heat and simmer until reduced to ⅓ cup (about 4 minutes). Refrigerate for at least 45 minutes or up to a day. Stir in orange juice. Pour into a 9- by 13-inch pan; cover and freeze for at least 2 hours or up to a month.

Break up mixture and whirl in a food processor or beat with an electric mixer until slushy. Serve immediately. Makes 4 to 6 servings.

RUE
(Herb-of-grace)

Ruta graveolens
Rutaceae (Rue family)
Perennial; hardy to –20°F/–29°C

Just one whiff of rue's powerful aroma and the word "medicine" springs to mind. And despite the occasional (and spare) use of rue in cooking, its herbal history is mainly medicinal.

From the time of ancient Greece through the Middle Ages, rue was thought to protect against magic and witchcraft. In the first century A.D., Pliny stated that consumption of rue helped preserve good eyesight, a belief that has endured through the centuries in Italy. Its folk name, herb-of-grace, may stem from the brushes made of rue that were once used in church services to sprinkle holy water.

Rue and its pungent scent figure in Europe's plague-ridden history. The aroma was believed to be both repellent and disinfectant, so sprigs of rue were used in prisons and courts of law to ward off germs and pestilence. As a strewing herb, it was employed for the same purposes.

Belief in such properties was reinforced when it was learned that rue was an ingredient in "four thieves' vinegar," a concoction drunk by thieves who robbed bodies of plague victims, yet failed to contract the disease.

DESCRIPTION. The word "fernlike" has aptly been applied to rue. The plant is a bushy perennial, decked out in soft bluish green leaves divided into numerous segments to produce a filigree effect like that of maidenhair fern. The foliage is aromatic, but the scent produced by merely brushing against it is often perceived as unpleasant — and the sap in the leaves and stems can cause a skin rash in susceptible individuals.

Rue plants are shrubby and more or less rounded, growing to 2 to 3 feet high and wide. In spring, clusters of ½-inch greenish yellow blossoms make a substantial show and then form seed capsules that have some decorative value when dry.

Two variant plants are fairly widely available from perennials and herb specialists. 'Jackman's Blue' makes a smaller plant, to about 1½ feet high, bearing distinctly bluish gray leaves; all plants are raised from cuttings.

Bluish green leaves irregularly splashed in cream and yellow are the feature of 'Variegata', which can be raised from seed as well as from cuttings.

CULTURE. Rue is a tough plant that will survive drought and poor soil. But it grows and looks better in average to good well-drained soil with moderate to regular watering. If your soil is decidedly acid, add lime when preparing soil to reduce acidity.

Cut back plants in early spring to encourage bushiness and pinch stem tips at any time to stimulate more branching. You can start plants from seed or from cuttings taken in late spring or summer.

HARVEST & USES. Nowadays, rue is chiefly a decorative herb, planted both for its contribution to garden beauty and for its dried seed heads, which are attractive in arrangements. Despite its medicinal history, avoid ingesting rue; in large doses it's toxic and skin irritation is always a possibility.

SAGE
(Garden sage)

Salvia officinalis
Labiatae (Mint family)
Perennial; hardy to –10°F/–23°C

At one time, garden sage was highly esteemed for its medicinal qualities. Cures attributed to it ranged from broken bones and wounds to stomach disorders and loss of memory. It was said of this herb, "How can a man die with sage growing in his garden?" Nowadays, we might ask instead how we could stuff poultry without sage!

DESCRIPTION. Garden sage is an attractive, shrubby plant that comes in several foliage and flower variations. Oval, 2-inch leaves with a pebbly surface cover a rounded plant to about 2 feet high and up to 3 feet across. In mid- to late spring, stems elongate into upright flowering spikes that present tiered clusters

of inch-long blossoms in a lovely shade of violet-tinted blue.

In the basic species, leaves are a soft gray-green, the model for the color sage green. Several selections offer different leaf colors. 'Icterina' has green leaves marbled with chartreuse to yellow. New leaves of 'Purpurascens' emerge a soft wine purple and age to gray-green; leafstalks and stems are purple. 'Tricolor' foliage is basically gray-green with irregular white margins, but new growth is tinged purple so the white portions appear pink.

A plant offered as 'Dwarf' grows to about 1 foot high, its leaves proportionately smaller. 'Berggarten' produces no flowers but offers significantly larger leaves of silvery gray with a covering of feltlike white hairs. 'Albiflora' features white blossoms on a plant outfitted in narrow leaves; 'Rubriflora' is its red-flowered counterpart.

CULTURE. Although garden sage is fairly drought tolerant, plants look better with moderate watering. Plant in full sun, where soil is well drained and of just average to even poor fertility.

You can raise the basic type from seed or start plants from cuttings of new growth in mid- to late spring. The variants are all perpetuated by cuttings.

After plants flower, cut them back; and in early spring, just as growth renews, cut plants back by about half.

HARVEST & USES. Garden sage, fresh or dried, is traditional in stuffings for meat and poultry and appears in many dishes of Mediterranean and Near Eastern origin. Use it also in making sausage, herb vinegar, and herb butter. Leaves retain the greatest amount of flavor when they're dried slowly.

Quick Foccacia

    3 cups baking mix (biscuit mix)
    2 teaspoons rubbed sage
    1 cup milk
    6 tablespoons olive oil
       Garlic salt

In a large bowl, mix baking mix and sage; stir in milk until blended.

Pour 2 tablespoons of the oil into a 9- by 13-inch pan; spread oil over bottom. Place dough in pan and pat into an even layer. With your fingertips, poke holes in dough at 1- to 2-inch intervals. Brush remaining oil evenly over dough; sprinkle lightly with garlic salt. Bake in a 400° oven until richly browned (about 25 minutes). Cut into rectangles. Makes 6 to 8 servings.

SAVORY

Satureja montana, S. hortensis
Labiatae (Mint family)
Perennial (*S. montana*), hardy to
–10°F/–23°C
Annual (*S. hortensis*)

As early as Roman times, the savories were recognized as stimulants, leading to one of their more interesting applications — as an aphrodisiac. Some offer this as the reason for Pliny's name for these plants, *satureia*, the name for the lusty, goat-footed satyr.

But the savories were also popular among the ancient Mediterranean cultures for the flavor they added to foods. Romans made a sauce with savory, and the savories were highly regarded as bee plants, from which excellent honey could be made.

DESCRIPTION. Perennial winter savory (*Satureja montana*) makes a fine-textured, shrubby plant to about 15 inches high, with ascending stems. The narrow leaves, ½ to 1 inch long,

Winter savory

grow opposite one another in pairs, each positioned at a right angle to the pair below. Small white to pale lilac flowers appear during summer.

Annual summer savory (*S. hortensis*) is a less-attractive plant growing a bit taller and more open in habit, with slightly larger leaves sometimes tinted with red. White to pink flowers come in summer.

CULTURE. Both savories are undemanding, easy-to-grow herbs. Winter savory prefers a well-drained, rather light or sandy soil and just moderate watering. You can grow plants from seed, but germination is slow; you may prefer to start with young plants in spring. Start new plants from cuttings in late spring and summer or from division of established clumps in early spring. Cut back plants as needed to maintain compactness.

Annual summer savory also prefers a fairly light, well-drained soil but one that has been well dug and amended with organic matter. Sow seeds in the garden; then thin seedlings to 12 to 18 inches apart. Water routinely.

HARVEST & USES. The two savories have a similar flavor — distinctly peppery with a dash of lemon — but summer savory is a bit softer and milder. Use leaves fresh or dried to season mild-flavored meats and fish, soups, egg dishes, cheeses, and vegetables. Add them to herb vinegars and salad dressings.

Indian Mixed Vegetables

¼ cup butter or margarine
1 medium-size onion, sliced
¼ teaspoon ground turmeric
1 large potato, peeled and cubed
1½ cups water
1 small head cabbage, shredded
1 small cauliflower, cut into small pieces
1 cup fresh or frozen, thawed peas
2 tomatoes, peeled and cut into wedges
1 bunch spinach, washed, coarse stems removed
1 tablespoon chopped fresh savory or ½ teaspoon dry savory
Salt

Melt butter in a 5- to 6-quart pan over medium-high heat. Add onion and turmeric. Cook, stirring, until onion is limp (about 5 minutes).

Add potato and water; reduce heat, cover, and cook for 5 minutes. Add cabbage and cauliflower; simmer, covered, for 5 minutes.

Stir in peas, tomatoes, spinach, and savory; cook, uncovered, for 3 to 5 more minutes.

Season to taste with salt.
Makes 12 servings.

SCENTED GERANIUMS

Pelargonium species
Geraniaceae (Geranium family)
Perennials; hardy to about
25°F/–4°C

These aromatic plants make up in charm what they lack in history. Related to the familiar geraniums (selections of *Pelargonium* x *hortorum*), these species have forsaken flashy flowers for olfactory delight, their scented leaves mimicking the aromas of other plants.

DESCRIPTION. Rose-scented rose geranium (*Pelargonium graveolens*) makes a sizable, shrubby plant in frost-free climates. Deep green, slightly hairy leaves have five to seven lobes, each further divided and toothed. The scent is pungent and spicy. Clustered flowers are rose colored or purple with pink veins. 'Rober's Lemon Rose' offers soft, gray-green lobed leaves that mingle the scents of rose and lemon. Mint-scented rose geranium (*P. g.* 'Variegatum') has creamy leaf margins. 'Attar of Roses', a selection or hybrid of *P. capitatum*, is an upright plant with finely cut, rough-textured foliage.

Peppermint-scented geranium (*P. tomentosum*) has velvety-surfaced lobed leaves to 5 inches across on a spreading, almost vinelike plant. Small white flowers come in fluffy clusters.

Other spice-scented kinds appear among the *P.* x *fragrans* hybrids. 'Nutmeg' has small, rounded gray-green leaves on a bushy plant bearing pink-veined white flowers; 'Snowy Nutmeg' has nearly gray leaves with cream margins; and 'Old Spice' is an upright plant with crinkle-edged grayish green leaves.

Lemon-scented geranium (*P. crispum*) has small, crinkly leaves on a 2- to 3-foot plant with lavender flowers. 'Prince Rupert' has larger, more strongly scented leaves and pink flowers; in 'Prince Rupert Variegated' ('French Lilac'), leaves are irregularly margined in cream. Orange geranium 'Prince of Orange' features larger foliage and white flowers. Lime-scented geranium (*P.* x *nervosum*) makes a bushy plant with ruffle-edged light green leaves and showy lavender flowers.

Apple-scented geranium (*P. odoratissimum*) has trailing stems to 1½ feet long clothed in roundish, ruffled leaves; white flowers form fluffy clusters. For an apricot scent, choose *P. scabrum* 'M. Ninon'; the bushy, 3-foot plant has glossy, dark green leaves and dark pink flowers.

A peach aroma appears in the small, crinkled leaves of *P. crispum* 'Peach Cream'. Foot-high *P. capitatum* 'Shotesham Pet' has red flowers and deeply cut, light green leaves with a filbert scent. Almond-scented geranium (*P. quercifolium* 'Pretty Polly') is a large plant with lobed, light green leaves and pink and crimson blossoms.

CULTURE. Tender scented geraniums are appropriate in the ground only in mild-winter regions, but they're quite content to grow in containers and spend the winter indoors. For growing out-of-doors, give plants a light, well-drained soil in sun to partial shade; water moderately. Pinch growing tips to encourage branching and remove spent flowers to prolong bloom.

New plants are easily started from cuttings taken during late spring and summer.

HARVEST & USES. Fresh leaves can impart their scent to jelly and iced drinks, dried leaves to potpourris and sachets.

Mint-scented rose geranium

SELF-HEAL
(Heal-all)

Prunella species
Labiatae (Mint family)
Perennials; hardy to
–20°F/–29°C

Herbalists were lavish in their praise of this herb's particular curative powers. According to the Doctrine of Signatures, the plant's throat-shaped flowers indicated its effacacy in treating diseases and complaints of the throat.

Thus, it's not surprising that the name *Prunella* is a metamorphosis of an old German word for tonsilitis. Culpepper, waxing enthusiastic on the plant's uses, explains the name self-heal: "When you are hurt, you may heal yourself" with the plant.

Self-heal was a noted wound herb, pressed into use to heal cuts, bruises, and ulcers. And Culpepper's enthusiastic description of its powers was scarcely an exaggeration. In the days before modern wound-dressing, stitches, and antibiotics, self-heal was, according to Culpepper, "an especial remedy for all green wounds to close the lips of them and to keep the place from further inconveniences."

DESCRIPTION. The self-heals are low-growing, spreading plants that will colonize an area with creeping rootstocks and by seed. In this habit, as well as in general appearance, they resemble their relative, carpet bugle (*Ajuga*), which is often used as a small-scale ground cover.

Although the leaf character is variable from species to species, the flower shape and carriage are the same. Flowers come in dense clusters at stem ends; each blossom is two-lipped, the upper part resembling a hood.

The most widespread self-heal is *Prunella vulgaris*, which occurs throughout much of Europe and adjacent Eurasia and has naturalized in North America and Australia. Attractive but somewhat weedy (a lawn weed in some regions), it reaches about 12 inches high when in flower. Leaves are oval to diamond shaped, up to 2 inches long; upright stems bear violet blossoms during summer.

A more attractive and less aggressive plant is *P. grandiflora*, sometimes called "large self-heal." Plants in flower reach 1½ feet high, with leaves twice the size of *P. vulgaris*. Individual purple blossoms are 1 to 1½ inches long and appear in 3-inch spikes; white- and dark pink–flowered forms sometimes are sold.

CULTURE. Give self-heal average to good soil where plants will receive full sun to partial shade. Best growth comes with routine watering, though *P. vulgaris* will persist despite lack of attention.

Set out plants in early spring. You can start new plants from cuttings, but by far the easier method is to remove rooted segments from an established clump. Volunteer seedlings of self-heal, *P. vulgaris* in particular, will keep you supplied with new plants.

HARVEST & USES. Self-heal is a relic of centuries-old folk medicine, grown nowadays for its historical associations and its beauty.

SORREL

Rumex species
Polygonaceae (Buckwheat family)
Perennials; hardiness varies

Both the kitchen and the dispensary have known sorrel for many centuries. Leaves have been chewed to quench thirst, made into a drink to reduce fever, and consumed to ward off scurvy. Topically, they were applied to counteract scabs, sores, boils, and ringworm.

As a salad herb, potherb, and basis for a popular meat sauce, sorrel has been familiar to Europeans for centuries. Immigrants brought the plant with them to the New World.

DESCRIPTION. Two species of sorrel are commonly grown. Larger of the two is common sorrel (*Rumex acetosa*; hardy to

−30°F/−34°C), also known as garden sorrel and sour dock. Leaves grow to nearly 6 inches long, many shaped like elongated arrowheads. Plants form foliage clumps from which rise leafy stems to 3 feet high, bearing insignificant flowers in summer.

In contrast, French sorrel (*R. scutatus*; hardy to −10°F/−23°C), also called garden sorrel, grows as a somewhat sprawling plant to perhaps 1½ feet high, the leaves shorter and broader than common sorrel and carried at the ends of long leafstalks.

Although both species are edible, French sorrel is less bitter with more definite lemony flavor than common sorrel and therefore is preferred for cooking.

CULTURE. Choose a sunny location with reasonably good soil for both sorrels. Common sorrel prefers regular moisture. French sorrel will tolerate some dryness, but, for a good leaf crop, water routinely.

Sow seeds in early spring for harvest starting a few months later, or set out young plants. Cut out flowering stems to encourage leaf production. Although the sorrels are perennials, replace (or dig and divide) plants after 3 or 4 years.

HARVEST & USES. Use leaves fresh or freeze them for later use in dishes where just flavor (and not leaf texture) is needed.

Use small amounts of fresh leaves in salads or cook the

leaves with spinach or cabbage. Add a fresh leaf of French sorrel to any cream soup during the last few minutes of cooking.

Creamed Sorrel

1 pound sorrel leaves (about 10 cups, lightly packed)
Béchamel Sauce (recipe follows)

Remove and discard tough stems and center ribs of sorrel. Wash well and drain.

In a 6- to 8-quart pan, bring 4 quarts water to a boil; drop sorrel into water and quickly push beneath surface. Drain immediately, submerge in cold water, and drain again. Set aside.

Prepare Béchamel Sauce. Add drained sorrel to warm sauce. Cook over medium-high heat, stirring, until hot. Makes 4 or 5 servings.

Béchamel Sauce. *Melt 2 tablespoons butter or margarine in a 1½- to 2-quart pan over medium heat. Add 2 tablespoons all-purpose flour and cook, stirring, until light golden (about 3 minutes).*

Remove from heat and stir in ½ cup each regular-strength chicken broth and half-and-half (light cream). Return to high heat and bring to a boil, stirring.

Season to taste with salt and freshly grated nutmeg.

SOUTHERNWOOD
(Lad's love)

Artemisia abrotanum
Compositae (Daisy family)
Perennial; hardy to –10°F/–23°C

Southernwood gained its name in England, which distinguishes it, a native of southern Europe, from the common wormwood found in the British Isles.

Quoting Dioscorides as authority, Culpepper makes claims for its use in treating an amazing range of conditions, including convulsions, eye inflammations, acne, worms, gangrene, and diseases of the spleen. Supposed aphrodisiac qualities account for the folk name, lad's love.

Southernwood's strong but rather pleasant scent was thought to be a germicide; thus, sprigs of the plant had a place in courts of law to protect against contagion from prisoners. And churchgoers might carry sprigs of it as a sort of smelling salts to revive them from sleep-inducing sermons.

As an herb tea, southernwood has been drunk as a general tonic; in Italy and parts of France, it has found limited culinary use. But the ever-practical French found a better — and still valid — use for the plant and gave it an appropriate name. Known as *garde robe*, it was hung in clothes closets to repel moths.

DESCRIPTION. Southernwood becomes a billowy mound of filigree leaflets that take a backseat only to fennel in delicacy. And, as an added bonus, the sage green leaves have a lemony scent.

Growth is spreading, with ascending stems to about 2½ feet high and greater spread if not restricted. Inconsequential greenish white flowers appear in elongated sprays during summer.

CULTURE. Southernwood is best when grown in full sun; it tolerates some shade, but plants are rangy and less attractive. Soil isn't an issue: good or poor will suffice, though good drainage is appreciated. Water moderately.

You can raise plants from seed, but it's simpler to set out small plants in spring. Thereafter, you'll have a ready supply of additional plants, since stems root here and there where they touch soil, cuttings root easily, and established clumps can be divided and replanted in early spring or autumn.

You can let southernwood spread at will, keep it somewhat contained as a rounded shrub, or trim it into an informal hedge. Cut back overgrown plants heavily in early spring; new growth will quickly fill in.

HARVEST & USES. Use southernwood for its fragrance, hanging sprigs of the plant among clothing as a moth repellent or tucking it into drawers of clothing and linens.

SWEET CICELY

Myrrhis odorata
Umbelliferae (Carrot family)
Perennial; hardy to −20°F/−29°C

Over the centuries, no one has had a bad word for sweet cicely. In fact, in what might sound like faint praise, the plant was touted in old herbals as "so harmless you cannot use it amiss." In the realm of medicine, however, it had a low profile, despite a recommendation for a decoction of its roots in wine as a treatment for consumption.

Sweet cicely's reputation rests on its value as an edible herb, a distinction that may seem strange for a plant that never shows up at the supermarket or in spice jars. Whether you use seeds, leaves, or roots, the flavor is sweet and somewhat licorice- or aniselike. As a sweetener in cooking, it may be valuable to persons trying to restrict their intake of sugar.

Crushed seeds are said to make a good furniture polish, imparting both gloss and scent to the wood.

DESCRIPTION. Sweet cicely is an especially lovely foliage plant and one you can enjoy for much of the year. It's among the first plants to leaf out in late winter or early spring and the last to lose leaves in late autumn.

Each lacy, delicate green leaf consists of a central leafstalk and secondary branches. These secondary branches bear deeply cut leaflets of descending size toward their tips, forming an outline like that of a Christmas tree. Light green and slightly downy, they turn purple in autumn before dying down for the year.

In summer, flower stems rise 3 to 4 feet high, bearing lacy, rather flat-topped clusters of small white blossoms. Elongated seed capsules that form after flowers fade point upward like clusters of fingers; they ripen to a brownish black color.

CULTURE. In cool-summer regions, you can grow sweet cicely in full sun, but where the climate is warmer, a position in semi- to full shade will encourage the best performance. Give plants reasonably good soil and routine watering.

You can start plants easily from seed, sowing it directly in the garden in autumn for germination the following spring. If you have an established plant, you can take root cuttings in early spring to increase your planting, though volunteer seedlings will usually abound if you let the plants go to seed.

HARVEST & USES. All parts of the plant are useful. Chopped raw leaves are tasty in salads, as well as in soups and egg dishes. Cooked with acidic fruits (such as rhubarb), sweet cicely reduces tartness and thus the amount of sugar needed to sweeten.

The unripe seed capsules have a sweet, nutty flavor that's appealing in fruit salads; the ripe seeds can be used in various cookies and pastries.

You can peel the roots and cook them as a root vegetable, slice them for stir-fries, or dice or shred them into salads.

SWEET WOODRUFF

Galium odoratum
Rubiaceae (Madder family)
Perennial; hardy to –20°F/–29°C

Sweet woodruff will win you over with its charm even before you succumb to its refreshing scent. Found in woodlands throughout much of the European continent, it figures in a number of pleasant customs that feature its aroma or flavor. It's probably best known as a flavoring of German May wine.

An unusual characteristic of the sweet woodruff new-mown-hay aroma is that it develops only when the plant is dried — and then the scent persists undiminished for years.

Naturally, then, this was a popular strewing herb in cen-turies past, and bunches of it were at one time hung in church-es to freshen the air. Stuffed into mattresses, it relieved the "tired" odor borne of long use.

At one time, sweet woodruff even had medicinal applications, particularly in treating disorders of the liver, kidneys, and repro-ductive organs. Steeped in water, the leaves made a tea that was not only pleasant but also seda-tive: an herbal tranquilizer.

DESCRIPTION. Many of to-day's gardeners enjoy sweet woodruff in its utilitarian role as a ground cover without ever real-izing that they're growing an his-torical herb.

Dense growth consists of nar-row, bright green, aromatic leaves that appear in closely set whorls on slender stems to 6 to 12 inch-es high. Creeping stems root as they spread, resulting in a carpet of foliage.

Tiny, four-petaled white flow-ers spangle this feathery cover in late spring and summer. At all times, a planting of sweet wood-ruff has a fresh appearance.

CULTURE. Sweet woodruff grows best in shaded locations where soil is good and slightly acid and moisture is assured. Un-der ideal conditions, the plant, in fact, can spread rapidly to the point of becoming invasive.

You can raise sweet woodruff from seed, but it's simpler to set out small plants in early spring. Thereafter, you'll always have a ready supply of new plants from volunteer seedlings and from rooted stems as they spread.

HARVEST & USES. The odor of newly mown hay develops only after the leaves of sweet woodruff are dried. Fortunately, you can harvest the leaves at any time, and they dry rapidly.

Use the dried leaves as a fla-voring in white wine, steep them in hot water for a refreshing herb tea, or include them in potpour-ris and sachets.

May Wine

- 4 bottles (750 ml. each) dry white wine
- 1¼ cups powdered sugar
- 12 sprigs sweet woodruff
- 1 cup brandy (optional)
- 4 cups chilled sparkling water or champagne
- Crushed ice

In a punch bowl, combine 1 bottle of the wine, sugar, sweet woodruff, and, if desired, brandy. Cover and let stand for 30 minutes. Remove sweet woodruff sprigs; reserve sev-eral for garnish. Add sparkling water and remaining wine; blend. Add ice. Garnish with reserved sprigs. Makes about 18 cups.

TANSY

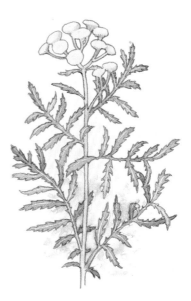

Tanacetum vulgare
Compositae (Daisy family)
Perennial; hardy to −30°F/−34°C

Ancient Greek legend tells of the abduction of mortal Ganymede by the god Zeus, who wanted the youth for a cupbearer to replace the disgraced Hebe. To confer immortality on Ganymede, he was given a drink made from tansy. Other accounts from antiquity suggest that tansy served as an important embalming herb. The very name tansy is said to derive from the Greek word for immortal.

From conferrer of immortality, tansy descended to quite mundane status in the centuries that followed the collapse of the Roman Empire. Its pungent odor called it into service as an insect repellent: bunches were hung in rooms, sprigs tucked into drawers, and stems strewn on floors. Tansy may even lay claim to being the world's first flea powder.

Taken internally, the herb was thought to be a good vermifuge for children and was also prescribed in cases of nervous afflictions, sluggish kidneys, and even gout.

Despite the plant's strong odor, tansy was once used as a culinary herb. Its pungency made it an adequate substitute for some of the more exotic and expensive Asian spices in cakes, puddings, and main dishes. During the Middle Ages and later, tansy cakes became a tradition at Easter to break the Lenten fast.

DESCRIPTION. In some old books, tansy is listed as *Chrysanthemum vulgare,* a now-invalid name that nevertheless indicates this plant's affinity to that large group of the daisy family. Compare tansy to feverfew (see page 57) and you'll notice the connection.

"Coarse" and "weedy" are words that have been used to describe tansy, though "robust" is just as accurate. The vigorous plants make spreading clumps of upright stems that may reach 3 feet high by flowering time.

The strongly aromatic bright green leaves consist of alternate, finely cut leaflets that give an overall ferny quality to the foliage. At the ends of stems in late summer come flattened clusters of buttonlike yellow flowers that actually are daisies without petals.

Fern-leaf tansy (*Tanacetum vulgare crispum*) takes the foliage to a further degree of ornateness. Individual leaflets are larger and more deeply cut (but less aromatic), giving the entire plant a more lush, fernlike appearance. Stems are shorter, reaching about 2½ feet high at flowering time; in cool-summer regions, plants may fail to bloom.

CULTURE. Given full sun, obliging tansy will grow in nearly any garden soil. Plants are somewhat drought tolerant, but appearance is better with moderate to routine watering. Clumps spread by creeping rootstocks and will need to be dug and divided frequently for rejuvenation — even annually if plants are grown in good soil with plenty of water.

HARVEST & USES. Tansy today is grown strictly for decoration and some insecticidal use. Dried flowering stems are attractive in arrangements.

Dried stems with foliage can be hung in rooms to discourage flies; dried leaves and sprigs placed in drawers may help repel insects and keep mice at bay.

TARRAGON

Artemisia dracunculus
Compositae (Daisy family)
Perennial; hardy to –10°F/–23°C

It may seem odd that such a non-descript plant as tarragon is associated with dragons. Yet both its common name (from the Arabic via Spanish) and its species name *dracunculus* (from Latin) mean little dragon.

Ancient use offers the explanation: tarragon was thought to cure bites of mad dogs and assorted venomous creatures. Both leaves and roots were once recommended to alleviate toothaches, while infusions of leaves were drunk to ease digestion.

DESCRIPTION. In contrast to the more elaborate, grayed leaves of southernwood and wormwood, *Artemisia* relatives, tarragon's narrow 2-inch leaves are plain, green, and glossy.

French tarragon

Two forms of the species exist; for cooking purposes, the distinction is important. The first, French tarragon (sometimes designated *Artemisia dracunculus* 'Sativa'), is a sprawling, largely flowerless plant with aromatic, flavorful leaves reminiscent of anise and mint. The plant slowly spreads by creeping rhizomes, the stems becoming slightly woody and the entire plant remaining less than 2 feet high.

Russian tarragon, the other form, lacks the characteristic aroma and flavor. It's sometimes identified as *A. d.* 'Inodorus' and is easily recognized by its upright, branching growth to about 3 feet, as well as by its small white flowers in late summer. Unlike French tarragon, Russian tarragon produces seeds (any tarragon seed you find for sale is the culinarily deficient Russian form).

CULTURE. Plant tarragon in good, well-drained soil where it will receive full sun or, in hot regions, a bit of afternoon shade. Give plants moderate to routine watering.

To maintain vigorous growth, divide and replant established clumps every 3 or 4 years. For additional plants, remove rooted segments from a clump's perimeter or take cuttings in summer.

HARVEST & USES. Fresh tarragon leaves have the strongest flavor, though dried leaves are satisfactory in cooking. To pre-serve fresh tarragon, freeze the sprigs airtight in plastic bags; or blend them with salad oil into a paste and freeze in small, rigid containers.

Tarragon is a versatile flavoring. Use it in vegetable and egg dishes; with chicken, lamb, veal, and fish; and in a variety of butter, cream, and cheese sauces. Its fresh leaves make a tasty vinegar.

Asparagus with Tarragon Vinaigrette

1½ pounds asparagus, tough ends removed
¼ cup white wine vinegar
¼ cup olive oil or salad oil
1 tablespoon chopped fresh tarragon or 1 teaspoon dry tarragon
Salt

In a wide frying pan, cook asparagus in ½-inch boiling water over medium-high heat until tender-crisp (about 7 minutes). Drain, plunge into ice water, and drain again. (At this point, you may cover and refrigerate for up to a day.)

Arrange asparagus in a rimmed dish. In a small bowl, mix vinegar, oil, and tarragon until blended; season to taste with salt. Pour over asparagus; turn to coat evenly. Makes 6 servings.

THYME

Thymus species
Labiatae (Mint family)
Perennials; hardy to –30°F/–34°C

Today, we associate thyme with food, but in antiquity, the herb was valued as an antiseptic. In fact, the Egyptians used it in embalming preparations. Even now you find thyme in embalming fluids, as well as in perfumes, oral-hygiene products, liqueurs, and, of course, a variety of foods.

DESCRIPTION. For centuries, the thymes have been cherished for their aromas and flavors. But all of them, from ground-hugging creepers to dense shrublets, are also charming plants for the foreground of any sunny herb garden or perennial border.

Common, or garden, thyme (*Thymus vulgaris*) is typical of the shrubby types; it possesses the classic thyme aroma and flavor. Plants make a rounded to spreading mound to 6 to 12 inches high, consisting of many

Silver thyme

branched stems and narrowly oval, ¼-inch gray-green leaves.

Tiny lilac flowers appear in dense whorls, sometimes nearly covering plants in summer. Widely sold is silver thyme (*T. v.* 'Argenteus'), which features silvery white leaf variegations.

Lemon thyme (*T.* x *citriodorus*) is as shrubby as common thyme but has slightly larger and broader leaves that pack a pungent, sweetly lemony punch when bruised or crushed. In spring, rounded heads of tiny rosy lavender blossoms nearly obscure the foliage. Two variegated forms are the most widely grown: 'Aureus' has bright green leaves edged in cream; 'Argenteus' features gray-green leaves margined in white.

Mother-of-thyme (*T. praeox arcticus*, sometimes sold as *T. serpyllum* or *T. drucei*) keeps its main stems flat to the ground but sends up branches from 2 to 6 inches high. Dark green, ¼-inch leaves are strongly aromatic; white or purplish white flowers appear in tufted clusters in summer. 'Reiter's' is a selection with rose-red blossoms.

Two species hug the ground. Caraway-scented thyme (*T. herba-barona*) has wiry stems and narrow ¼-inch leaves that emit a caraway scent when crushed. Clustered blossoms are rose pink. Woolly thyme (*T. pseudolanuginosus*), the lowest-growing of all, forms an undulating mat to 2 to 3 inches high. Tiny, rounded

leaves are gray and woolly. Small pink flowers usually are sparsely produced.

Specialty herb growers may offer other thyme plants, all well worth growing.

CULTURE. Thymes need well-drained soil and moderate watering. Where summers are cool to mild, plants thrive in full sun; in hot-summer regions, provide light afternoon shade.

You can raise common thyme from seed, but most other thymes are set out as young plants in spring or summer. Shear or cut back established plants to maintain compactness. Stems usually self-layer, ensuring replacements, but cuttings also root easily in spring and summer.

HARVEST & USES. A popular culinary herb, thyme is good with poultry, fish, and pork; in sauces and soups; and in vinegar. It's one of the ingredients in Italian herb seasoning. Use sprigs fresh for an attractive garnish. Dry or freeze leaves for winter use or grow plants in pots indoors for a steady supply. To make a jelly with thyme, see Apple-Herb Jelly on page 106.

VALERIAN
(Common valerian, garden heliotrope)

Valeriana officinalis
Valerianaceae (Valerian family)
Perennial; hardy to –30°F/–34°C

Cats find valerian as hypnotically alluring as catnip. And, by odd coincidence, valerian's odor has the same effect on rats. It's even been suggested that the Pied Piper of Hamelin owed his success not to his enchanting flute music but, instead, to roots of valerian hidden in his clothing.

The old folk name for this plant, all heal (not to be confused with self-heal), suggests the usefulness of valerian as a medicinal herb in the centuries before prescription medicines. In particular, it had a reputation for efficacy in treating a variety of nervous disorders, claims that have been validated by modern research.

Valerian has a sedative effect on the central nervous system, providing relief from nervous stress, insomnia, and some migraines. In the 16th century, it was recorded as a cure for epilepsy. During World War I, valerian was administered both to shell-shocked troops and to distraught civilians. And, of course, valerian has a history of effective use as bait in rat traps.

Note that the related plant, *Centranthus ruber*, also goes by the name valerian. In western North America, where winter temperatures remain above 0°F/–18°C, it appears as an attractive roadside weed; its flowers are white, pink, or dusty red.

DESCRIPTION. Valerian has tall, straight stems to about 4 feet high when in flower, well above the bulk of the leaves, which remain fairly close to the ground. Each leaf consists of 8 to 10 pairs of narrow, opposite leaflets with conspicuously jagged edges.

Flowering stems are sparsely leafed, elongating in summer to bear branched clusters of tiny pink blossoms; white- and red-flowered forms also exist.

CULTURE. Grow valerian in good soil where it will receive sun to partial shade and regular watering. You can start plants from seed, but this herb is easily grown from divisions of established clumps.

Spreading rootstocks may crowd nearby plants in time. You can dig and divide congested (or overly aggressive) clumps in early spring.

HARVEST & USES. Nowadays, valerian is an herb to appreciate for its useful past. Grow it for the decorative contribution it makes to the garden. Flowering stems are attractive in fresh arrangements.

VIOLET
(Sweet violet)

Viola odorata
Violaceae (Violet family)
Perennial; hardy to –10°F/–23°C

It's no wonder that the praises of violets have been sung by writers from ancient times to the present. Who wouldn't love these seductively fragrant flowers that seem to peer at one from among their leaves?

Ancient Greeks regarded violets as a symbol of fertility. Romans drank a wine made of violet flowers. Both Hippocrates and Pliny, anticipating the medieval Doctrine of Signatures, recommended wearing a chapelet of violets to counteract a wine hangover. For treatment of gout, Pliny also endorsed a concoction of violet root in vinegar.

Early inhabitants of the British Isles employed violets in primitive cosmetics. A syrup of violet flowers was promoted by the herbalists for a variety of conditions, including epilepsy, insomnia, jaundice, and constipation.

Violets even have a political history. France's Emperor Napoleon I, during his years in exile, was referred to in code by his loyal supporters as "Caporal Violette." Upon his return to the throne, the violet became the emblem of the Napoleonic Party.

DESCRIPTION. Sweet violets are among the first flowers to assure gardeners that spring is coming. An established violet patch will, in fact, remain colorful—and eye-catching—for more than a month.

An individual violet plant consists of a clump of long-stalked, heart-shaped to nearly round leaves. Plants grow to just 4 to 8 inches tall and increase like strawberries, sending out runners that root and produce new plants at their tips.

Because of their low stature and spreading nature, violets make excellent small-scale ground covers beneath deciduous shrubs and trees; they're also good edging plants along pathways in shaded herb gardens.

Flowers come on stems just long enough to rise above the foliage. Purple is the typical color, but you can find selections with flowers in blue, white, pink, or wine shades. And sweet they are; most exude the fabled violet fragrance, perfuming the air around the planting.

Perennials specialists and herb growers carry named selections in the various colors.

CULTURE. Where summers are cool, you can plant violets in full sun. Otherwise, the hotter the summer, the more shade they'll need. Set out plants in good soil liberally enriched with organic matter.

You can dig and separate old clumps in early spring for increase; with faster-growing selections, you may need to curb the spread periodically by removing the clump's perimeter. Volunteer seedlings may further increase your supply.

HARVEST & USES. Sugared violet flowers (see page 106) make an elegant and tasty decoration on cakes, pastries, and other desserts. Fresh violet blossoms are a lovely garnish for salads and contribute color and intriguing flavor to vinegar. Dried flowers add their scent to potpourri and sachet.

WORMWOOD

Artemisia species
Compositae (Daisy family)
Perennials; hardy to –30°F/–34°C

Use of wormwood can be traced back to ancient Egypt. But today, wormwood may best be remembered for having been a component of the addictive liqueur absinthe, the drink that led to the demise of Toulouse-Lautrec (among others) and which was said to have been responsible for so grisly a murder in France that manufacture of the product was banned there.

Another alcoholic spirit still contains wormwood and even bears its name: vermouth is but the French rendering of the German word *wermuth*, which means wormwood.

Common wormwood

The bitter essence of wormwood, strongest in common wormwood (*Artemisia absinthium*), accounts for its historic use as a medicine and insect repellent. Since ancient times, it has been recommended as a vermifuge. And later, claims were made for wormwood's effectiveness in treating stomach disorders, lack of appetite, digestive upset, nervous conditions, and even seasickness. One purported gout remedy was an infusion of wormwood flowers aged in brandy.

The secret to medical success lay in proper dosage. Used with discretion and care, wormwood was supposed to be effective; taken in excess, it could provoke toxic reactions, including epileptic-type convulsions and damage to the central nervous system.

DESCRIPTION. Several different *Artemisia* species go by the name wormwood, and two have long-standing herbal histories.

The common wormwood of alcoholic-beverage notoriety is an upright, branching, shrubby plant to 2 to 4 feet high, bearing finely divided silvery gray, silken-surfaced leaves. Their odor is pungent, their taste bitter. Tiny grayish flowers appear in summer in airy, branched spikes at branch tips. 'Lambrook Silver' is a fine selected form that grows to just 2½ feet high.

Roman wormwood (*A. pontica*) reaches a height similar to common wormwood, but leaf segments are slightly more fine, and flowers are yellowish white. In comparison, its aromatic leaves are noticeably less pungent. Plants form spreading clumps from a creeping rootstock.

CULTURE. Neither wormwood is particular about soil fertility, but both need a soil that is well drained. Moderate watering is sufficient.

Cut back plants fairly heavily just before the growing season begins; this will keep growth compact and plants well clothed in leaves. You can start new plants from cuttings in spring and summer; established clumps can be divided in early spring.

HARVEST & USES. The wormwoods are valued chiefly for their decorative contribution to the herb garden.

You can pick sprigs of common wormwood to use as an insect repellent in closets and drawers.

YARROW

Achillea species
Compositae (Daisy family)
Perennials; hardy to –30°F/–34°C

The botanical name of these plants, *Achillea*, pays homage to ancient legend. The Greek warrior Achilles, battling the Trojan forces, is said to have used yarrow leaves to stem the flow of blood from his soldiers' wounds. Whether the story is true or not, these plants do have a history of use in treating cuts and wounds.

Diverse claims were made for teas and infusions of yarrow leaves. A tea, for example, was reputed to cure or alleviate a cold and was also drunk to overcome melancholy. Washing the head with yarrow water was touted as a prevention for baldness. To take away the pain of toothache, simply chewing a yarrow leaf was supposed to suffice. And in the brewing of beer and ale, yarrow replaced hops in some Scandinavian preparations.

DESCRIPTION. All yarrows have tiny flowers grouped in flat-topped clusters at the ends of stems; leaves generally are narrow and divided into numerous segments.

Common yarrow (*Achillea millefolium*), sometimes referred to as "milfoil," has 3-foot stems that range from upright to sprawling; they're clothed in narrow, gray-green, very finely divided leaves that give a fernlike effect (*millefolium* means thousand leaves).

Flowers are white in the basic species, but named selections include pink-flowered 'Rosea' and red-flowered 'Cerise Queen', 'Fire King', and 'Red Beauty'. The Galaxy series of hybrids offers a range of colors, including pink shades, crimson, and buff.

The tallest yarrows are selections and hybrids of fernleaf yarrow (*A. filipendulina*). 'Coronation Gold' (to 3 feet) and 'Gold Plate' (to 5 feet) are widely available. Another popular yarrow is 2-foot-high A. 'Moonshine', its lemony yellow flowers appearing above silvered gray-green foliage. Reaching about the same height, A. *taygetea* features sulfur yellow flowers that fade to soft yellow; leaves are gray-green.

Three low-growing yarrows make good foreground plants and small-scale ground covers. Greek yarrow (*A. ageratifolia*) forms spreading mats of silvery gray leaves above which 1-inch clusters of white flowers come on 10-inch stems. Silvery yarrow (*A. clavennae*, formerly A. *argentea*) is of similar size but offers pale cream flowers. Woolly yarrow (*A. tomentosa*) is green leafed with yellow flowers; 'King George' (cream) and 'Primrose Beauty' (light yellow) are named selections.

CULTURE. Given full sun and periodic division, yarrows can be counted on for good performance with little care. They grow best in good, well-drained soil but will perform decently in poorer soils as long as drainage is good. Moderate watering is best, but established clumps will tolerate quite a bit of drought. Divide crowded clumps in early spring.

HARVEST & USES. Although the yarrows are now primarily decorative plants, you can use chopped leaves — sparingly — in salads. Dried flower heads are a favorite in arrangements.

Common yarrow (Galaxy hybrids)

USING HERBS FROM THE GARDEN

Whether you're drawn to herbs because of their intriguing and ancient histories, because of the distinctive flavors they contribute to food, or simply because of their beauty in the garden, the desire to use the herbs you grow is bound to surface. You'll be surprised at how easy it is to steep them into refreshing teas, blend them into delicious spreads for bread or crackers, or preserve them for use in potpourris or floral arrangements. Best of all, finding ways to use herbs allows you to bring their beauty, taste, and fragrance into your home to enjoy year-round.

Cloaked in ripe bittersweet berries, a barn houses the products of the year's herb harvest: dried herbs for cooking, scent, and decoration, and a variety of herb vinegars

HARVEST & PRESERVATION

Whether you intend to use your herbs fresh or dried, for cooking, for scent, or for indoor decoration, it's important to know when to pick them so they're at the peak of their flavor. And when you preserve herbs by drying, freezing, or packing them in salt, you can enjoy that flavor even during the coldest months of the year, when fresh herbs may not be readily available.

HARVESTING FRESH HERBS. Because herbs tend to lose some of their flavor during the drying process, you'll want to harvest fresh herbs when flavors are at peak development.

Gathered into bunches and hung upside down in a shaded spot, herbs dry in the same way that they have for centuries.

For herbs in which the flavor is in the foliage, prime picking time usually is when flowers start to open. At that stage, the oils that give each herb its distinctive quality are most concentrated. Exceptions to this rule are sage leaves, which you pick when buds first appear, and hyssop, lavender, rosemary, and thyme, which are at their best when plants are in full bloom. For harvesting, choose a sunny, dry morning just after the dew has evaporated from the leaves but before the sun becomes hot enough to volatilize the essential oils.

When your harvest objective is a seed crop for culinary use — for example, anise, caraway, coriander, or dill — wait until the seed heads are browned but not quite fully ripened so the seeds don't scatter. The simplest procedure is to cut entire seed heads or seed-bearing stems into a paper bag; after drying, you can winnow seeds from chaff on your kitchen table.

To harvest flowers for drying, choose newly opened blossoms that are fresh and bright.

DRYING LEAVES, SEEDS & FLOWERS.
Although sunlight is drying, it destroys some of the herb flavor that you're trying to preserve. The best natural drying methods simply expose leaves, seeds, and petals (or simple whole flowers) to freely circulating air that is warm and dry. (Drying flowers this way, though, can rob them of their color; for an alternate drying method that preserves floral color, see the section on preparing potpourri ingredients on page 108.)

The most picturesque drying method entails hanging bunches of cut herbs upside down. This works best with herbs that you can cut with long stems, such as marjoram, some mints, rosemary, sage, and savory. After cutting the stems (leave the leaves attached), rinse them and remove any dead or discolored leaves. Tie the stem ends together into small bunches and hang them in a warm, dry place away from direct sunlight. Make sure air can circulate freely around them. If you dry bunched herbs outside (in a shady spot), take them indoors at the end of the day so nighttime dew won't dampen them.

To prevent dust from settling into the drying herbs, you can place the bunches inside paper bags. Gather the top of the bag around the tied stem ends so leaves hang freely inside. Cut out the bottom of the bag and make holes in the sides for ventilation.

The drying process takes a few weeks. When leaves are crackly dry, carefully remove them from the stems, leaving the leaves intact, if possible.

To dry large-leafed herbs, flowers (either petals or simple whole flowers), or short tips of stems, spread them — leaves attached or stripped away — in a single layer on trays and place them in a warm, dry location away from sunlight. (Simple wooden frames with bottoms of window screen or cheesecloth are excellent as drying trays and are easy to make.) Every few days, gently stir or turn the herbs to assure thorough drying. Remove them from the trays when they're crisp-dry.

Dry seeds in the same way, spreading the seed heads in a shallow layer; remove them when individual seeds are ready to separate from the dried seed capsules.

To dry leaves in a hurry, you can microwave them. Place several stems on a double layer of paper towels, cover with a single layer of toweling, and microwave at full power (100%). Small-leafed herbs, such as rosemary and thyme, should dry in about 2 minutes; the larger-leafed kinds take about 3 minutes.

STORING DRIED HERBS. Choose airtight containers for storing your thoroughly dried herbs. Leaves retain flavor longer if you store them intact and break them up only as you use them. All herbs lose flavor if they're exposed to light (through glass containers) or heat. The best storage places are in cool cupboards or even in the refrigerator.

During the first week after you package your dried herbs, check to see if any moisture has condensed inside the container. If so, remove the herbs for further drying; otherwise, they'll decay in storage.

FREEZING FRESH HERBS. Freezing softens the leaf tissues, but it doesn't alter flavor.

Because some herbs discolor when frozen, some directions call for blanching and then quick-cooling the herbs before freezing. But color hardly

Simple screened frame functions as a drying rack for a shallow layer of leaves, petals, and whole flowers.

matters when herbs are used in cooking, so the easiest method is simply to wash the fresh herbs and shake them dry, remove the leaves from the stems, and place them in freezer bags; seal the bags tightly and label them. With larger-leafed herbs, you may want to chop the leaves before freezing them. For cooking, use the leaves directly from the freezer.

PRESERVING HERBS IN SALT. This old-fashioned method gives you herb-flavored salt as a by-product. First, rinse the leaves and let them dry or blot them dry with a cloth or paper towel. Then remove the leaves from the stems. Pour a layer of noniodized salt (or sea or kosher salt) into a jar, add a layer of leaves, and cover with another layer of salt. Continue alternating layers, pressing down firmly, until the jar is full. Cover tightly and store in a cool, dark place.

To use salt-cured leaves, remove them as needed and rinse to remove the salt; or take the salt into account in cooking.

HERBS IN EDIBLE PREPARATIONS

Throughout the world, herbs play a central role in flavoring both food and drink. The use of herbs in cooking and baking may be very familiar to you; included here are some additional ways you can put herbs to work in the kitchen. For specific suggestions for each herb, see the encyclopedia beginning on page 33.

To ensure a supply of herbs the year around, preserve them in one of the ways discussed on pages 102–103.

COOKING WITH HERBS. Most cooks regularly use herbs, fresh or dried, in recipes. In fact, certain foods have become so closely identified with the herbs that customarily flavor them that it's difficult to imagine the food without the herb.

Throughout the growing season, pick just healthy leaves, never those yellowed or browned with age. Use them whole or chopped, as specified in the recipe. As plants gain in size, you'll be able to cut sprigs of young growth from the ends of stems, thereby promoting bushier growth in the process.

HERB TEA. Nothing could be simpler to prepare than an herb tea: you just add boiling water to your chosen herb leaves.

Flavor varies, according to the herb used, from refreshing to almost medicinal. Some of the most popular herb teas are brewed from bee balm, chamomile, lemon balm, lemon verbena, and mint. But you can brew a tea from almost any of the culinary herbs. Intensity of flavor depends on the amount of herb you use for brewing.

Experiment to determine the right amount for your taste. Begin by trying about 2 teaspoons fresh herb (or 1 teaspoon dried herb) for each 6-ounce cup water. Put the herb in a tea ball or directly into a teapot and then add boiling water. Most herb teas are best if steeped for at least 10 minutes, but beware of steeping too long, as the herb may become bitter. For stronger flavor, increase the amount of herb used rather than the steeping time. Strain the tea, if desired.

HERB VINEGAR. Herb-flavored vinegar gives an extra flavor boost to any dish that calls for vinegar in the recipe. You can make the vinegar from a single herb — tarragon or dill, for example — or

Aromatic fresh herbs, alone or combined with spices, turn ordinary wine vinegar into a culinary treat.

choose some compatible herb combinations. Use fresh, washed sprigs (you'll need about 4 long sprigs for about 3½ cups vinegar). Petals of edible flowers, such as roses, and many spices also make flavorful vinegars.

The bottle you use should have a tight-fitting screw top, stopper, or cork. Put the ingredients of your choice in the clean bottle and fill it with plain white or red wine vinegar. Cover tightly. Label the bottle and let it stand undisturbed in a cool, dark place for at least 3 weeks so flavors can develop. Once opened, the vinegar should be stored in a cool, dark place (or refrigerated) and used within 4 months.

HERB HONEY. Just as the pollen source can influence a honey's flavor (think of clover, alfalfa, and eucalyptus honeys, for example), so can the addition of herbs. Among the herbs you can try are mint, lemon verbena, scented geraniums, thyme, and sweet cicely. Use about 1 tablespoon chopped fresh herb or 1 teaspoon dried herb to 1 pint bland honey.

Combine the herb and honey in a small pan over low heat; stir only until the honey becomes warm. Pour the mixture into a clean jar, cap tightly, and store in a dark place at room temperature for about a week. Return the mixture to a pan, warm it, and strain out the herbs. Rebottle.

HERB BUTTER OR CHEESE. Using either fresh or dried herbs, you can turn butter or cream cheese into a seasoned spread for breads and rolls, crackers, and vegetables.

Simply combine about ⅓ cup fresh herb or 2 tablespoons dried herb with ½ cup softened butter or cream cheese in a blender or food processor; whirl until blended. Or finely chop fresh herbs or crush dried herbs in a mortar and pestle and then beat them into the butter or cheese until smooth. Cover and refrigerate for up to 2 weeks or freeze for up to a month.

HERB SALT OR SUGAR. To infuse salt with the flavor of a particular herb, simply follow the directions on page 103 for preserving herbs in salt. By substituting sugar for salt, you can have sugar with an herbal accent.

Snippets of chives contribute mild onion flavor to this cream cheese, used as a simple spread for French bread.

To make herb salt in an instant, combine 1 cup noniodized salt (or sea or kosher salt) with 4 to 8 tablespoons dried herbs. Whirl in a blender until fairly uniform. Store airtight.

SUGARED FLOWERS & LEAVES. Delicate flowers and leaves, sparkling with a coating of sugar crystals, elegantly flavor cakes, pastries, frozen desserts, even bowls of punch and glasses of champagne. Among flowers, violet and borage are favorites for sugaring; leafy herbs for this treatment include lemon balm, scented geraniums, and mint.

Pick fresh flowers and leaves, rinse them, and gently pat dry. While they air-dry, separate 1 egg, placing the white in a small bowl (reserve the yolk for other uses). Beat the egg white until frothy;

using a pastry or artist's brush, brush the beaten white onto flowers and leaves just to moisten all surfaces. Sprinkle with fine granulated sugar. Arrange on wax paper in a shallow tray and let stand in a dry, warm place for several days. Transfer to an airtight container and refrigerate.

HERB JELLY. Combining fruits — or even sugar alone — with herbs creates jellies and jams that add a piquant note as spreads on toast, rolls, even waffles; some can double as condiments with entrées, such as the familiar combination of mint jelly and lamb.

The herb jelly recipes below require no processing. Store them in the freezer or refrigerator.

Sparkling, starlike borage blossoms can be transformed into charming decoration for desserts by the simple process of sugaring.

Lime-Mint Jelly

    8 to 10 limes
    4 cups sugar
 1¾ cups water
       Green food coloring (optional)
    1 pouch (3 oz.) liquid pectin
    3 tablespoons finely chopped fresh mint

Rinse unpeeled limes. Grate thin outer peel (colored part only) from 5 limes; set aside. Squeeze enough limes to make ¾ cup juice.

Pour lime juice, sugar, and water into a heavy-bottomed 8- to 10-quart pan and stir until well blended. Bring to a boil over medium-high heat, stirring occasionally. Stir in enough food coloring, if desired, to get desired color.

Stir in pectin all at once. Add grated lime peel and mint. Bring to a full rolling boil; boil, stirring, for 1 minute. Remove from heat and skim off any foam.

Ladle hot jelly into freezer jars or freezer containers, leaving a ½-inch headspace; apply lids. Let stand for 12 to 24 hours at room temperature. Freeze for up to 1 year or refrigerate for up to 1 month. Makes about 5 half-pints.

Apple-Herb Jelly

    2 cups bottled filtered unsweetened apple juice
  ¼ cup dry thyme, ⅓ cup dry basil, 2 tablespoons dry
       rosemary, or ¼ cup dry mint
    3 tablespoons lemon juice
 3½ cups sugar
    1 pouch (3 oz.) liquid pectin

In a heavy-bottomed 6- to 8-quart pan, bring apple juice to a boil. Remove from heat, stir in thyme, and cover. Let stand for 30 minutes (or 2 hours for basil; 15 minutes for rosemary; 10 minutes for mint). Pour mixture through a jelly bag or a cheesecloth-lined colander. Squeeze out and reserve liquid; discard herbs. Rinse pan; return liquid to pan. Stir in lemon juice and sugar. Bring to a boil over high heat, stirring constantly. Pour in pectin all at once, bring to a full rolling boil, and boil, stirring, for 1 minute. Remove from heat and skim off any foam.

Process hot jelly as described for Lime-Mint Jelly (at left). Makes about 4 half-pints.

Garlic Jelly

  ½ cup finely chopped garlic
       About 3 cups white wine vinegar (5% acidity)
 1½ cups water
    6 cups sugar
    2 pouches (3 oz. each) liquid pectin

Combine garlic and 3 cups of the vinegar in a 2- to 2½-quart pan. Bring to a simmer over medium heat; simmer gently, uncovered, for 15 minutes. Remove from heat; pour into a glass jar. Cover and let stand for 24 to 36 hours at room temperature; then pour through a fine strainer into a bowl, pressing garlic with back of a spoon to squeeze out as much liquid as possible. Discard residue. Measure liquid; if necessary, add vinegar to make 2 cups or boil liquid to reduce to 2 cups.

In a heavy-bottomed 8- to 10-quart pan, mix flavored vinegar, water, and sugar. Bring to a full rolling boil over medium-high heat, stirring. Stir in pectin all at once, return to a full rolling boil, and boil, stirring, for 1 minute. Remove from heat and skim off any foam.

Process hot jelly as described for Lime-Mint Jelly (at left). Makes about 7 half-pints.

POTPOURRI & SACHET

While many herbs have individually appealing aromas, you can become a sort of magician with nature's scents when you combine a variety of dried herbs and flowers into fragrant mixtures.

Potpourri

Increasingly popular today are colorful potpourris that evoke romantic images of a simpler life in earlier times. Any potpourri is no more than a mixture of fragrant flower petals, select herbs and spices, and a fixative — the combination preserved in an attractive bowl or container. (A closed container that you open for an occasional whiff will retain more of the aroma for a longer period than an open container.)

Although in popular usage the word "potpourri" has come to mean a medley or mixture, it's derived from two French words that, freely translated, mean rotting pot, a somewhat apt if unappealing reference to potpourri made by the moist method. Both the moist method and the somewhat simpler dry version, though, use the same ingredients.

Potpourri-making is much like cooking: you experiment with ingredients until you get a result you like. The "recipes" on page 109 are presented only as a starting point. Experiment with the aromatic herbs in your garden, following the guidelines below.

BASIC COMPONENTS. The main ingredients of potpourri are generally dried flower petals and aromatic leaves. Rose petals and lavender blossoms are traditional; the various pinks can also be used for their clovelike scent. For suitably fragrant roses, let your nose be your guide. A number of the old-fashioned "heritage" roses are powerfully fragrant, but don't overlook modern hybrids, such as 'Double Delight', Fragrant Cloud', 'Chrysler Imperial', 'Granada', 'Mister Lincoln', 'Perfume Delight', and 'Tiffany'.

Leaves from a number of herbs can contribute a variety of scents. Good choices include basil, bay, bee balm, chamomile, lemon balm, lemongrass, lemon verbena, marjoram, mint, oregano, rosemary, sage, scented geraniums, sweet woodruff, tarragon, and thyme. Even certain herb seeds, such as anise, caraway, coriander, and fennel, can contribute to the mix.

From the world of spices, you'll find potpourri ingredients in allspice, cinnamon, cloves, ginger, mace, nutmeg, and vanilla bean. Citrus peel (the

The very word "potpourri" conjures up the scent of rose petals, stored here in glass jars ready for mixing with other ingredients.

Potpourri mix (at left) includes woolly betony (lamb's ears), rose petals, lavender blossoms, orris root, plus globe amaranth flowers for color and rose oil for additional scent. Chopped orris root (above) is a traditional fixative and scent.

and sandalwood. Purchase these oils from specialty herb craft suppliers. The various cooking extracts and flavorings you find in the supermarket aren't satisfactory in potpourris.

Because their aromas are so concentrated, use essential oils very sparingly, adding them by the drop to the fixative rather than directly to the mixed potpourri.

PREPARING THE INGREDIENTS. Choosing freshly opened flowers and mature herb leaves, harvest your herbs and dry them as described on pages 102–103; for potpourri, you can strip leaves off stems and petals from flowers before drying, especially if the flowers contain many petals packed together. Note that for moist potpourri, you only need to dry the materials partially; they should feel leathery rather than crisp-dry.

If you want to retain some of the color of the flower petals, important if the potpourri will be stored in a clear glass container, you can dry whole blossoms of certain flowers that will remain colorful, among them bee balm, borage, elecampane, nasturtium, pot marigold, and violet. To dry whole flowers, spread borax or fine sand about ½ inch thick in a box. Place flowers face down; sift more borax or sand over them until they're covered. Set the box in a warm, dry place until flowers are dried (at least 2 weeks).

DRY POTPOURRI. Following one of the recipes on the facing page or using your own combination, place the dried leaves and petals in a large bowl. Gently mix them until they're well combined. Blend in additional spices and seeds a little at a time while you assess the fragrance you're creating. Finally, add the fixative (to which you've already added any essential oils of your choice). Lightly toss. Place the mixture in a glass or ceramic container and tightly cover. Let the mixture stand for 5 to 6 weeks to blend; shake or stir the potpourri periodically during that time.

After the maturing period, fragrances should be blended and set. Add colorful dried whole flowers, if desired, and put the mixture into decorative containers. For longest-lasting aroma, cover the containers.

colored part only — either chopped or shredded— is another familiar component.

All potpourri recipes call for a fixative, which serves to absorb the essential fragrant oils and retard their evaporation. Some fixatives even contribute a bit of their own fragrance to the final product. They generally come powdered or ground; either is suitable, but the powdered forms won't look as good in glass containers since they tend to coat the insides.

Two commonly used fixatives are orris root (see page 78) and gum benzoin; look for them in health food stores, herb shops, or pharmacies. Others include calamus powder, storax, tonka beans (vanilla scented), and vetiver root. As a general rule, add 1 to 1½ ounces (roughly 2 to 3 tablespoons) fixative for every 4 cups petals and leaves.

Manufactured essential oils are optional ingredients you can incorporate to give your potpourri a memorable but not quite identifiable fragrance. Typical are oils of such flowers as carnation, jasmine, lavender, orange blossom, rose, and violet, as well as more exotic scents like myrrh, patchouli,

Summer Harvest Potpourri

8 cups (2 quarts) dry rose petals
1 cup each dry lemon verbena and dry rose geranium
½ cup dry lavender blossoms
¼ cup each dry bee balm, dry rosemary, and finely chopped and dried orange peel
3 tablespoons coarsely ground orris root
2 tablespoons crushed gum benzoin
1 tablespoon tonka beans, cut
1½ teaspoons each whole cloves and dry coriander seeds, crushed

Assemble ingredients as directed for dry potpourri (see facing page).

All-Herb Potpourri

2 cups each dry pineapple mint and dry apple mint
¼ cup each dry bee balm, dry basil, dry lemon balm, dry lemon verbena, dry marjoram, dry rosemary, dry spearmint, dry sweet woodruff, dry clary sage, dry garden sage, and dry pineapple sage
3 tablespoons dry lavender blossoms
2 whole cardamom seeds and pods, crushed
10 dry coriander seeds, crushed
2 tablespoons powdered orris root

Assemble ingredients as directed for dry potpourri (see facing page).

Mixed Bouquet Potpourri

4 cups mixed dry flowers, such as calendula, clove pinks, lavender, and rose petals
1 cup dry bay leaves
¼ cup chopped orris root
½ teaspoon jasmine, rose, or lavender essential oil

Assemble ingredients as directed for dry potpourri (see facing page).

Moist Rose Petal Potpourri

8 cups (2 quarts) dry rose petals
  Dry lavender blossoms and dry basil, dry marjoram, dry pineapple sage, and dry rosemary
  Coarse noniodized salt
1 tablespoon nigella seed
1 to 2 tablespoons chopped and dried tangerine peel (colored part only)
1 teaspoon each ground cinnamon, ground mace, ground nutmeg, and ground ginger
12 whole cloves, crushed
2 tablespoons powdered orris root
5 drops orange blossom, patchouli, or rose geranium essential oil

Assemble ingredients as directed for moist potpourri (see below).

MOIST POTPOURRI. Compared with the dry potpourris, those made by the moist method tend to have a stronger aroma and to retain the scent much longer, often for many years (provided the container is tightly stoppered most of the time). The process removes all color from the petals and leaves, so moist potpourris are best stored in opaque containers.

Place the partially dried leaves and petals in a large, straight-sided crockery jar in ½-inch layers, alternating with sprinklings of coarse noniodized salt. Pack the mixture firmly. When the jar is three-quarters full, place a nonmetallic weight on top of the mixture to keep it packed down. When moisture drawn out by the salt rises to the top, stir the petals and let them cure, undisturbed, for 10 days; the petals will form a moist cake.

Break up the cake very finely and blend it with spices and seeds; add the fixative (with added essential oils, if desired). Place the potpourri in an opaque, covered container.

Sachet

What separates sachet from potpourri is the packaging. Potpourri is traditionally kept in jars, crocks, or open containers, often decorative pieces. Sachet, on the other hand, is contained in small packets so it can be tucked away in drawers of linens and personal garments to perfume the contents.

Sachets can be simple or elaborate. One way to make a simple sachet is to place dry potpourri in the center of a handkerchief, gather up the corners, and tie them with a ribbon. More complicated projects involve making small packets or pillows from fine fabric and stuffing them with dry potpourri crumbled to a fairly fine texture.

DECORATING WITH HERBS

With their varied colors and textures, dried herbs can become handsome wreaths and bouquets for household adornment at any time of year.

HERB WREATH. Multipurpose creations, dried herb wreaths make attractive holiday alternatives to the more standard wreaths of holly and conifer boughs. Laid flat on a table, they become instant centerpieces. If you choose your herbs deliberately, the wreath can eventually be retired to the kitchen, where its components will end up in future meals.

For wreath-making, you need a simple wire frame (look for frames in crafts shops or make your own), florist's wire, and dried herbs with stems long enough to wire to the frame. Herbs that you've dried upside-down in bunches work best, including bay, germander, lavender, lavender cotton, marjoram, rosemary, rue, sage, southernwood, wormwood, and yarrow. You can add variety to the mix by including other favorite dried materials or such decorative elements as ribbons and pinecones.

Shorter-stemmed herbs can be poked into a hard foam ring until its surface no longer shows.

HERB BOUQUET. Arrangements of dried herbs can introduce beauty and aroma to any room of the house. Just as with fresh flowers, bouquets can be huge show-stopper creations for special occasions or small tabletop arrangements of, say, lavender and wormwood.

The most attractive bouquets employ contrasts in texture and form. In addition to the herbs listed above for wreath-making, try dried stems and seed heads of anise, caraway, dill, fennel, mullein, purple coneflower, and rue; and dried rose hips.

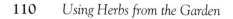
Design: Chrissie Grady.

Romantic herb wreath (at left) includes California bay, lavender cotton, rosemary, wormwood, and dried rose blossoms. Decorative but utilitarian garlic braid (below) is enlivened with dried blossoms of yarrow and ornamental annual plume cockscomb (Celosia).

HERBS & THEIR USES

Herb	Edible	Tea	Scent	Household
AGRIMONY		Flowers Leaves Stems	Flowers Leaves Stems	
ANGELICA	Leaves Stems Roots	Leaves	Leaves Roots	Seeds
ANISE	Leaves Seeds	Leaves	Seeds	Seed heads
ANISE HYSSOP	Leaves	Leaves		
BASIL	Leaves Stems		Leaves	
BAY	Leaves		Leaves	Stems
BEE BALM	Flowers Leaves	Leaves	Flowers Leaves	
BETONY, WOOD		Leaves		
BETONY, WOOLLY			Leaves	
BORAGE	Flowers Leaves		Flowers	
BURNET	Leaves	Leaves		
CARAWAY	Leaves Seeds Roots		Seeds	Seed heads
CATMINT	Strictly ornamental			
CATNIP	Leaves	Leaves		Leaves
CHAMOMILE		Flowers	Flowers Leaves	
CHERVIL	Leaves			
CHICORY	Flowers Leaves Roots			
CHIVES	Leaves			
CLOVE & COTTAGE PINKS	Flowers		Flowers	
COMFREY				Leaves Stems
CORIANDER	Leaves Stems Seeds		Seeds	
COSTMARY	Leaves		Leaves	Leaves
DILL	Leaves Seeds			Seed heads
ELECAM-PANE	Roots		Flowers Roots	
FENNEL	Leaves Seeds Roots	Seeds	Seeds	Seed heads
FEVERFEW	Strictly ornamental			
FOXGLOVE	Strictly ornamental			
GARLIC	Bulb			
GERMAN-DER	Strictly ornamental			
HORE-HOUND	Leaves	Leaves		

Herb	Edible	Tea	Scent	Household
HORSE-RADISH	Roots			
HYSSOP	Leaves			
LAVENDER	Leaves		Flowers	Flowers Stems
LAVENDER COTTON				Stems
LEMON BALM	Leaves	Leaves	Leaves	
LEMON VERBENA	Leaves	Leaves	Leaves	Leaves
LOVAGE	All parts			
MARJORAM	Leaves	Leaves	Leaves	Stems
MINT	Leaves Stems	Leaves Stems	Leaves	
MULLEIN				Seed heads
NASTUR-TIUM	Flowers Leaves Seeds		Flowers	
OREGANO	Leaves		Leaves	Leaves
ORIENTAL HERBS	See pages 76–77.			
ORRIS ROOT			Root	
PARSLEY	Leaves Stems			
POT MARIGOLD	Flowers Leaves		Flowers	
PURPLE CONE-FLOWER				Flowers Seed heads
ROSE	Flowers		Flowers	Hips
ROSEMARY	Leaves		Leaves	Stems
RUE				Stems Seed heads
SAGE	Leaves		Leaves	Stems
SAVORY	Leaves			
SCENTED GERANIUMS	Leaves		Leaves	
SELF-HEAL	Strictly ornamental			
SORREL	Leaves			
SOUTHERN-WOOD				Stems
SWEET CICELY	All parts			Seeds
SWEET WOODRUFF	Leaves	Leaves	Leaves	
TANSY				Flowers Stems
TARRAGON	Leaves		Leaves	
THYME	Leaves		Leaves	
VALERIAN				Flowers
VIOLET	Flowers		Flowers	
WORM-WOOD				Stems
YARROW	Leaves			Flowers Stems

INDEX